choice time

How to Deepen Learning Through **Inquiry** and **Play**, PreK–2

Renée Dinnerstein

HEINEMANN
Portsmouth, NH

Heinemann
361 Hanover Street
Portsmouth, NH 03801–3912
www.heinemann.com

Offices and agents throughout the world

The author and publisher wish to thank those who have generously given permission to reprint borrowed material:

Categories of play are derived from *Crisis in the Kindergarten: Why Children Need to Play in School* by Edward Miller and Joan Almon. Copyright © 2009 by Alliance for Childhood. Published by Alliance for Childhood. Reprinted with permission from the publisher.

Next Generation Science Standards is a registered trademark of Achieve. Neither Achieve nor the lead states and partners that developed the Next Generation Science Standards was involved in the production of, and does not endorse, this product.

Library of Congress Cataloging-in-Publication Data
Names: Dinnerstein, Renée, author.
Title: Choice time : how to deepen learning through inquiry and play, preK–2
/ Renée Dinnerstein.
Description: Portsmouth, NH : Heinemann, [2016] | Includes bibliographical
   references.
Identifiers: LCCN 2016029347 | ISBN 9780325077659
Subjects: LCSH: Early childhood education—Activity programs. | Inquiry-based
   learning. | Play.
Classification: LCC LB1139.35.A37 D56 2016 | DDC 372.21—dc23
LC record available at https://lccn.loc.gov/2016029347

Editors: Zoë Ryder White and Katie Wood Ray
Development editor: Alan Huisman
Production: Vicki Kasabian
Cover and interior designs: Suzanne Heiser
Typesetter: Kim Arney
Manufacturing: Steve Bernier

Printed in the United States of America on acid-free paper
20 19 18   VP   3 4 5

for Simon

Contents

> Tell me and I forget, teach me and I may remember, involve me and I learn.
>
> —Benjamin Franklin

How to Use This Book

I wrote this book with two major goals in mind: I want to show what a powerful, authentic, inquiry-based choice time could achieve when placed at the heart of an early childhood classroom. In addition, I want to give teachers everything they would need to implement choice time centers.

How This Book Works

The book is divided into two parts. Part 1 begins with "Why Choice Time and Play Are Important." This chapter presents the research on why play is important and what children can achieve through play as well as a description of the different types of play. The second chapter, "The Classroom Speaks," gives practical ideas for classroom arrangement, lists important materials, and offers suggestions for scheduling choice time in grades preK through 2. The last chapter in Part 1, "A Classroom Where Centers Thrive," focuses on the management of choice time—how to plan for centers, implement predictable routines, and use the workshop model. I also answer some questions that teachers frequently ask.

Part 2 focuses on what I might often call the meat and potatoes of choice time. It includes six chapters that present centers that will most likely be regular centers in your classroom. I describe the reasoning behind each center, show how to set it up, and list materials you'll need to begin. I also give ideas for introducing the center, provide some helpful minilessons, and suggest useful changes to keep things fresh across the year. This section of the book provides a practical template that can be used for observing, reflecting, and planning next steps in each center.

If you are a teacher new to choice time, you might want to use the centers just as I've described them and eventually take off on your own. If you've been using choice time already, I hope that this book gives you some new ideas for variations on your existing centers. In either case, I hope that you will heed the central lesson of this book, which is to tailor the centers to the interests of the children in *your* classroom. A child's engagement is the most powerful asset we have for teaching and learning.

You can continue a conversation about choice time with me and with other teachers by visiting my blog at investigatingchoicetime.com and sharing your ideas and experiences. I look forward to hearing from you!

Foreword

I first met Renée Dinnerstein in the mid-'90s when I was a research assistant
at the Teachers College Reading and Writing Project (TCRWP). My job was to
go to classrooms all over New York City and surrounding areas, day after day,
to observe teachers and children engaged in reading workshops. Then I'd head
back to the Reading and Writing Project to share findings and observations;
this was the time when the TCRWP was morphing from an organization focusing on writing to one that included reading instruction. On a résumé, this would
be viewed as a great job, but for an aspiring teacher, a job that enabled one
to work with colleagues at the TCRWP and in classrooms like Renée's was an
extraordinary gift.

When Lucy Calkins sent me to Renée's classroom at PS 321 in Brooklyn, she
told me to watch everything closely because I could find gold there. One day, I
had my times mixed up and I arrived early, well before Renée's reading workshop was to begin. She invited me in, explaining that it was choice time. My
choice to go in that day changed everything! From that day forward, I made
sure I *always* arrived at Renée's classroom early because I did not want to miss
the wonder of choice time in her kindergarten. I had struck classroom gold!

During choice time, Renée was often hard to find as she sat alongside children, observing, nudging, and supporting their approximations as they made sense of their world and their learning through their play. Her room was abuzz. There was a lot of action and conversation, but no signs of chaos or conflict. I eavesdropped on and observed children paired up on fluffy cushions, reading together inside a cozy refashioned and beautifully painted refrigerator box; children zooming small trains along subway maps as they taught themselves about directions and puzzled out map symbols together; and a small group working on a model of a suspension bridge that spanned a portion of the classroom while another group built cities in the block area. During any given choice time, there was a kaleidoscope of work and play— children cooking snacks, making plays, creating art, observing the class turtle, and so on. On the surface, it looked seamless and almost effortless, like all of the moving pieces just fell into place, but I always wondered, "How does this happen? What did Renée do?"

I tried to find moments to ask Renée questions or tell her about the striking things children were doing and saying, but it wasn't easy to have those conversations during class time because when children were in the room, they were Renée's focal point. The children were (and are) her priority, and they always had her undivided attention. Fortunately, we now have this book in which Renée takes us behind the scenes to the belief systems and planning that lead to robust, engaging, child-centered choice times. As I read it, I felt like I was finally having the conversation I longed to have back in the days when I observed in her classroom. In this book, Renée shares the secrets and stories of choice time so that any teacher might be able to create these authentic, engaging learning opportunities for his or her own students.

When I was looking to teach, Renée was one of the main reasons I applied for a position at PS 321. I wanted to work alongside teachers like her. We were colleagues at PS 321 for several years. Renée's presence in grade-level meetings was always grounding. She thought of the children first, no matter what. Renée served as any group's conscience, helping us stay rooted in the real needs of our students as we weathered ever-escalating expectations and occasionally became enamored by the latest teaching fads and tangled up in education buzzwords like *rigor*, *stamina*, and *standards*. Through her questions and her actions, Renée always reminded us that our true work was to teach *children*, not to teach stuff.

Even though she was more seasoned and experienced than many on our grade level, Renee modeled humility and vulnerability. She asked questions, she shared problems, and always, she remained steadfast in keeping children first and foremost. I learned from Renée the important but simple truth that teaching isn't about *us*, the teachers, but it's about doing what's right for *them*, the learners. I imagine you can detect a theme here.

Over the years, in my work as a consultant, I've asked teachers to think of resources they couldn't live without in their professional lives, including three people, three places, and three things. In other words, "Who and what have influenced you and continue to fuel you as a teacher?" If I were to answer this myself, I would name Renée. Our paths have crossed frequently, from the first time I researched in her classroom, to my years as a teacher at PS 321, to the cobblestone streets of Reggio Emilia, Italy, when I had the incredibly good fortune to participate in a study tour that Renée and Matt Glover had organized, to our shared hotel room at an NCTE conference, when we both felt exhausted and perplexed by the lights and noise of Las Vegas.

Through all of our shared experiences, Renée has become a cherished friend. I admire so much about her and her family, and I realize that not only is she one of my professional heroes, but she is a personal inspiration, as well.

As you read on in this book, you'll know what I know: Renée is a tireless and vocal advocate for the role of play, inquiry, and choice in early childhood classrooms, even when the education climate is storming with corporate reform, classroom rigor, and curricula on steroids. She has worked in schools all over, supporting teachers across the grades as they launched inquiries and created choice times in their classrooms. In this capacity, Renée empowers teachers with whom she works, as many of them have presented stories from their classrooms at local and national conferences.

And now, Renée has empowered us all by writing a book that matters so much. By sharing research and classroom anecdotes, Renée has given us a rationale for and a vision of choice time that can be transferred and tailored to any classroom. Even if you have never had the pleasure of watching Renée at work in her own classroom, you'll find that she writes in the same way she teaches, side by side with you, working tirelessly to get it right, staying true to her values, and always, always keeping her eyes on children.

—Kathy Collins

> Stand aside for a while and leave room for learning, observe carefully what children do, and then, if you have understood well, perhaps teaching will be different from before.
>
> —Loris Malaguzzi, The Hundred Languages of Children

Why Choice Time and Play Are Important

Some years ago, my daughter visited my classroom during choice time. Observing the children at play—turning the dramatic play corner into a doctor's office, constructing spaceships from toilet paper rolls and egg cartons at the art table, using a screwdriver to take apart a broken telephone at the science center, using tubes and funnels to "invent" a machine at the water table—she said, "I feel like I'm walking into *King of Hearts*!" In this French movie set during World War I, alerted to an oncoming invasion, villagers flee to the countryside, accidentally leaving the gates of the town asylum open. The asylum residents wander about the town in wonder and amazement, happily assuming the jobs of the absent villagers. Although they understand some aspects of these roles, they add their own sometimes comical interpretations as they attempt to re-create what they perceive to be life in the outside world.

That morning in my classroom, my daughter observed children engaged in activities where they had the opportunity to imagine in very big ways. During choice time, children have the freedom and opportunity to try out ideas, seek answers, test predictions, navigate new social interactions, and experiment with a variety of materials in both structured and unstructured ways. *I'm going to see how many Unifix cubes it takes to go all around the classroom. I bet it will be more than a hundred!* As they play, children imagine themselves to be scientists, artists, doctors, mathematicians, architects, and inventors as they design and construct imaginary worlds. *We made a plan to build a spaceship. Here's our drawing. It has all the important parts because I found a diagram of a spaceship in a space book. Now Ian and I are going to build it with blocks.*

Children's play during choice time is literally fueled with imagination, and as Sir Ken Robinson (2006) has noted, "creativity is putting your imagination to work, and it's produced the most extraordinary results in human culture." Young children, of course, put imagination to work instinctively. They don't need anyone to teach them how to invent games and make up stories. They're naturals! In fact, as Diane Ackerman has observed, play is a natural part of life for all animals (except ants), and across species, play "invites problem-solving, allowing a creature to test its limits and develop strategies" (2000, 4). Through play, children learn the social mores that help them succeed in life (Brown 2010).

Early childhood educators have always understood the importance of play—in all its many forms—in the lives of their students. *Free play* is spontaneous and

Figure 1.1. Building a boat in the block center

filled with make-believe as children pursue the fantasies of their unencumbered imaginations (Hirsh-Pasek and Golinkoff 2003). A twig becomes the sword of a swashbuckling pirate, or a piece of flowing fabric is transformed into a super-hero's cape or the gown of a fairy princess. Free play is entirely child directed and free of adult intervention.

The play my daughter observed in my classroom is what is sometimes called *guided play* (Hirsh-Pasek et al. 2008). Guided play takes place in a purposeful environment that's been carefully planned to stimulate and support children's curiosity and creativity. As students interact with one another and the materials, teachers observe, record, confer, occasionally participate, or facilitate, and they use this information to plan next steps. However, the *children* decide how they will explore and interact with the materials, not the teachers. Although both types of play are important for the developing child, this book focuses on implementing inquiry-based, guided play in the classroom.

During choice time, children choose to play in a variety of centers around the room. Each center has been carefully designed and equipped to support play and inquiry that will nurture children's growth and development. The materials and activities in each center change over time in response to students' needs and interests and the academic focus of the curriculum. Examples of common centers are dramatic play, art, science, math, building (blocks and Legos), and music.

Recognizing and Honoring the Many Forms of Play

Before they ever come to school, children naturally learn and grow as they play with each other and with adults. This learning is essentially effortless—a natural consequence of play. Seeing this, it just makes sense that developmentally appropriate practices in classrooms should tap into the natural energy of play that children bring with them to school. In a 2012 position paper, the National Association for the Education of Young Children (NAEYC) notes the many benefits of children's play to developmentally appropriate practice. To clearly see each of these benefits in action, all you have to do is picture the children playing in the imaginary doctor's office on the morning my daughter visited my classroom (see pages 101–102). As the NAEYC paper notes, children's play has a number of advantages:

- *It helps develop self-regulation.* Children take turns playing different roles at different times. One child wants to be the doctor *now*, but she has to wait her turn.
- *It promotes the development of language.* Drawing from their experiences, the children support each other in using the particular language of a doctor's office: *fever, X-ray, medicine.*
- *It promotes cognition.* All the children must *think* their way through the play in very intentional ways. *I am in a doctor's office. What should I do next?*
- *It promotes social competence.* As children execute a successful play experience together, each of them is empowered by the role she or he plays in its success.
- *It gives children opportunities to explore the world.* In dramatic play particularly, children bring the world into their play, where they can explore it safely. Today it's a doctor's office; next week it might be a camping expedition or a fire station.
- *It provides opportunities for children to interact.* It's difficult to play "doctor's office" by yourself, so children must interact and co-construct all the meaning and decision making.
- *It provides opportunities for children to express and control their emotions.* All sorts of emotional issues can arise in play: fairness, inclusion and exclusion, a lack of understanding, varied expectations, success and failure.
- *It helps children develop their symbolic and problem-solving abilities.* Two chairs placed side by side make an examination table. But wait—it's not long enough for the "patient" to lie down on. *Let's get two more chairs!*
- *It gives children opportunities to practice emerging skills.* The doctor writes a prescription, carefully sounding out the words, "Pills for a cold."

The bottom line is, when children are at play, they're not just playing—they're learning. Play is the engine that drives their learning.

Play in Challenging Times

Given the clear, unequivocal position on play as developmentally appropriate practice by the NAEYC, you might think time for play is a given in early childhood classrooms everywhere. Unfortunately, opportunities for play are disappearing from children's lives, both inside and outside school. Early childhood teachers who believe strongly in the efficacy of play are often thwarted by today's education climate. Common Core State Standards, teacher ratings, and high-stakes testing draw our attention away from what we know is best for children. Running records and math assessments eat up hours of classroom time. The advocacy group Alliance for Childhood published a scathing report, *Crisis in the Kindergarten*, documenting the harm being done by transforming "public kindergarten from places where love of learning was thoughtfully nurtured into pressure-cooker classrooms where teachers are required to follow scripts, labor under unrealistic one-size-fits-all standards, and test children relentlessly on their performance" (Miller and Almon 2009, 15). It goes on to say that kindergarten has "ceased to be a garden of delight and has become a place of stress and distress" (15).

Stress and distress, of course, have developmental implications that extend beyond the classroom. In 2012, the American Academy of Pediatrics published "The Importance of Play in Promoting Healthy Child Development and Maintaining Strong Parent-Child Bond: Focus on Children in Poverty." The article warns:

> To effectively preserve play in the lives of economically disadvantaged children, its presence in schools . . . must be supported. In schools, the need to support social and emotional learning and healthy child development must be held alongside the need to increase academic scores. Otherwise, school engagement might suffer and efforts at creating a better-prepared generation might fail. (Milteer, Ginsburg, and Mulligan 2012, 209)

Is it possible for a teacher of young children to support social and emotional learning and healthy child development alongside academic learning, especially in the face of so many outside pressures? I believe it *is* possible and that a play-based curriculum best supports children across a wide spectrum of development. When planned thoughtfully, provocative and enriching centers can support and enhance reading, writing, mathematics, and phonics curriculum and also give children opportunities to be playful, self-directed, creative thinkers. The chapters that follow will help you imagine possibilities for these kinds of centers, but first it's important to understand the nature of play itself and all the ways curriculum might be developed with a focus on play. After all, as teachers, it's important that we are specific as we articulate, implement, and share with families, administrators, and classroom visitors the important learning that takes place while children are working playfully at their centers.

The Many Forms of Play

If you think again about the classroom scene my daughter witnessed on the morning she visited my classroom, it would be easy to label the children's actions simply as *play*, as in, "Look, they are playing." *Play*, however, is a very general term that can refer to a whole range of actions. In fact, almost anything, if undertaken in a playful spirit, could be called play and would come with all the benefits outlined earlier. But different types of play require different kinds of thinking, actions, and interactions. When planning for play-based curriculum, it's important to be very clear about these differences because they help us see ways to tie play to specific academic areas.

In describing what play should look like in kindergarten, *Crisis in the Kindergarten* (Miller and Almon 2009) distinguishes between twelve categories. Three of them—rough-and-tumble play, risk-taking play, and gross motor play—take place mostly outdoors and are outside the scope of this book. (For more information about recess and outdoor play, see the 2010 book *Playing for Keeps: Life and Learning on a Public School Playground*, by Deborah Meier, Brenda S. Engel, and Beth Taylor). The other nine types of play encompass the forms of exploration that support children's social, emotional, creative, and intellectual growth.

Artistic Play

In artistic play, children use a variety of materials to create and symbolically express both personal and aesthetic ideas. A well-equipped art center might include everything from clay to drawing tools to collage supplies. The thinking children do in artistic play is focused very specifically on the potential of different materials. It's possibility oriented—*What could I paint with these acrylics and that large blank paper?* (see Figure 1.2)—and children often revise their thinking as they play. Artistic play might also spring up spontaneously in other centers. For example, a child exploring leaves in a science center might decide to paint a picture of a tree in full autumn color.

Figure 1.2. What could I paint?

Sensory Play

Play that specifically engages a child's senses—touch, taste, sight, smell, hearing—is sensory play. Sensory play involves thinking about similarities and differences (*This one is rough; that one is smooth.*) and also connections (*This pencil eraser smells sort of like cinnamon.*). A center might be devoted specifically to exploring with one or more senses, but sensory play will also be incorporated into so many other kinds of play. Finger painting, for example, is artistic play but it's also very sensory in nature. Children exploring seashells will naturally feel them and notice the different textures, and children sorting coins might smell their different metallic odors. Children playing at a water or sand table will have lots of opportunities to heighten their senses.

Fine Motor Play

When children work on puzzles, sew pillows or dolls, string beads into necklaces, and sort materials at the science and math centers, these are all forms of fine motor play. Fine motor play helps children gain control over the mind-hand

Figure 1.3. By threading a needle, this kindergartner is also refining his motor skills.

relationship—*How do I get this thread through that hole?* (see Figure 1.3)—and develop the skills necessary for writing and drawing and all sorts of other work and life tasks. Centers of all kinds might purposefully include possibilities for fine motor play, and of course unplanned opportunities spring up naturally as well (a screw falls off a microscope and has to be reattached, for example).

Rule-Based Play

Because they are based on rules, card games and board games engage children in a particular sort of thinking that's different from their thinking in most other kinds of play. A child playing Candy Land or crazy eights has to follow steps, understand predetermined goals, and use complicated strategies to play the game. And of course there is the added dimension of winning and losing that can color all the thinking associated with rule-based play. You can include card and board games in different centers, but you can also invite children to invent their own games and then teach other children the rules and strategies they will need to play.

Mastery Play

When children learn to construct buildings without the blocks constantly crashing, they master the skill of balance. If a child can follow a predrawn plan and construct a bridge with K'Nex as designed, she has mastered how to use those materials intentionally. In mastery play, children use a process of thoughtful trial and error to stay with a skill until they've mastered it. Children who engage in mastery play are necessarily projecting their thinking into the future. They know if they just keep trying and doing, they will eventually get it. Mastery play is likely to be incorporated into all kinds of other play, depending on the different skills the play entails.

Construction Play

Construction play is exactly what it sounds like: it's any play that involves building! A block area, of course, is the classic place for construction play. With blocks of all sizes and shapes, children work with clear intention to build all sorts of structures, from boats to bridges to skyscrapers. The design-oriented thinking children use during construction play is rich and multifaceted. They solve problems and develop language skills as they collaborate. The unit configuration of the blocks (one long block equals four smaller blocks, and so on) helps them internalize mathematical concepts, recognize symmetry, and understand balance, weights, and angles. While a block center is specifically devoted to construction play, children might also build sets for plays or puppet shows or construct furniture for imaginary houses in dramatic play.

Make-Believe Play

Make-believe play can spring up anywhere in the classroom anytime the energy of play turns toward *Let's pretend. . . .* Having built a spaceship in blocks, children will naturally make believe they are astronauts traveling to other planets. Even children manipulating pattern shapes or counters in a math center might suddenly decide the shapes are jewels and they are pirates who've just made away with them. A dramatic play center, of course, is designed for make-believe play and is equipped with a variety of props that suggest different imaginative scenarios. As children make believe, their thinking is rich as they incorporate fantasy, practice saying new words, negotiate social relationships, and solve problems.

Symbolic Play

Symbolic play involves using one object to represent another. For example, a child who holds up a wooden block, declares, "This is a lion," and then roars loudly is engaging in a form of symbolic play, connecting fantasy and reality. Children sometimes engage in symbolic play for its own reward, but most often they incorporate it into other types of play. For example, the same block that was a lion "just for fun" might quite purposefully become a cell phone during make-believe play and be used to call 911. At some level, most artistic play is also symbolic. A child who paints a flower on a canvas or sheet of paper is creating a visual symbol for a mental image of something she may have seen in a garden or a flower store (or simply imagined). By creating symbols during various types of play with a variety of unstructured materials, children internalize the relationship between symbol and reality necessary to comprehend the symbolic language of print (Cohen 1988).

Language Play

Anyone who's ever watched a roomful of children erupt into uncontrollable laughter just because someone said, "There's a wocket in my pocket," knows that children love wordplay. When they experiment with rhymes, repetitions, and funny combinations of words, tell stories, and sing songs, particularly songs they've made up, children are playing with language and also developing mastery of the many workings of words. Language play springs up naturally as children play together in different centers, and it's not unusual to hear them use language creatively and uniquely as they experiment with new words, hum songs, or describe rules for a game.

Ideally, in a single day at school, a child would experience play—and the thinking and experience that come with play—in many different forms as he engaged with the carefully planned centers in his classroom. Children from prekindergarten through second grade can engage purposefully in all these different types of play as long as teachers are thoughtful about increasing sophistication and depth as children mature. Kindergartners and second graders might both experiment playfully with magnets, for example, but the second graders will build on past experiences and be expected to demonstrate increased complexity and profundity of thought.

To better understand how children naturally engage in different forms of play, you might observe a group of children engaged in free play over a period of time, say ten or fifteen minutes. Keep a running record of what they are doing and saying, and then try to label the different actions by the forms of play they represent: artistic, sensory, fine motor, rule-based, mastery, construction, make-believe, symbolic, or language. What do you notice? Are there patterns? Did one play form dominate the session? Do some children seem drawn more to certain forms of play?

Considering How Children Are Different

Understanding different types of play is important to the development of play-based curriculum, but so is understanding how children experience play in different ways. A little close observation is all it takes to begin thinking about how children bring different strengths, interests, and tastes to their play. Watch a busy classroom over time, and you'll notice the child who always takes the lead in organizing make-believe scenarios. You'll see the child who prefers to work quietly alone (see Figure 1.4) or in very small groups, drawn to anything he can observe closely. Another child is always giving his classmates advice on how to make things work more efficiently, and another is drawn to any play where she can move and make a little noise.

In teaching reading or mathematics, we differentiate instruction based on the needs of each student, and the same differentiation is essential to a play-based curriculum. When planning centers, we must consider our students' needs and capacities for interacting with materials and one another. Howard Gardner's theory of multiple intelligences is a helpful frame for thinking about the different ways children engage in play, and a play-based curriculum is most effective when it supports the strengths and proclivities of multiple intelligences.

Figure 1.4. Aubrey spends some time alone writing.

In *Frames of Mind*, Gardner describes nine different intelligences and explains, "In ordinary life . . . these intelligences typically work in harmony, and so their autonomy may be invisible. But when the appropriate observational lenses are donned, the peculiar nature of each intelligence emerges with sufficient (and often surprising) clarity" (2011, 9). Every child has the capacity to integrate more than one of the intelligences. However, individual children usually exhibit an intuitive strength in one of the intelligences over the others. When planning centers, it's helpful to consider how different learners will benefit from particular centers and also how centers can be open enough to support a variety of learning intelligences. Let's consider each of these now with an eye toward how the different intelligences might be supported in a play-based curriculum.

Linguistic Intelligence

Children with high linguistic intelligence are drawn to both spoken and written language. They enjoy using language to express themselves and to make things happen in the world. An ABC center, a writing center, and a poetry center all specifically support written language, but you might also consider having paper and markers in all centers so children who are drawn to writing can make notes, signs, and messages connected to their play. For spoken language, dramatic play centers provide many opportunities for children to play with words, make up stories, and use language for a variety of purposes. Children with high linguistic intelligence may also enjoy acting, creating puppet shows, or keeping a notebook of thoughts and ideas.

Musical Intelligence

A child who exhibits musical intelligence will be particularly sensitive to the many sounds in the environment and will be drawn to musical patterns. These children enjoy centers where there are opportunities to experiment with rhythm instruments and where they can create and record their own compositions (see the child writing her own music in Figure 1.5). Musical intelligence can be supported in other centers as well. If a class is investigating birds, for example, you might introduce a listening center where children can hear and identify various bird songs. You can encourage children to add background music as they act

Figure 1.5. Creating an original composition in the music center

out stories or make up songs to help them learn number patterns. Basically, any ways you can imagine having children incorporate sound or song into their play will support musical intelligence.

Logical-Mathematical Intelligence

Children with high logical-mathematical intelligence quickly recognize patterns, solve problems, and interpret graphs of information more abstractly. Math centers certainly support logical-mathematical intelligence, but you can also think about ways to embed math and problem-solving opportunities into other centers. You might place a tape measure in the block center, for example, or a calculator in the imaginary store. Children with logical-mathematical intelligence also enjoy applying logic to their questions and will delight in a survey center where they can interview classmates, gather and interpret data, and then create a document—perhaps a graph or pie chart—to illustrate their findings.

Spatial Intelligence

Children with high spatial intelligence enjoy figuring out possibilities for how space might be used—arranging furniture, designing the layout of a village built with blocks, organizing shelves and storage. Using spatial intelligence, a child sees perspective in a painting or understands that a story or a piece of writing is made up of distinct parts. Any materials that support children in planning or designing can be incorporated into centers to bolster spatial intelligence—even storyboards in the dramatic play area!

Bodily-Kinesthetic Intelligence

Gym and outdoor recess are the highlights of the day for children with high bodily-kinesthetic intelligence! These children need to move around, and they enjoy physically active art or construction projects over physically passive activities. They gravitate toward dramatic play or block-building centers. Once you understand and appreciate children's bodily-kinesthetic intelligence, you can use it to help them engage more thoughtfully with all kinds of content. Some children who might never choose a math center, for example, will go happily to an indoor hopscotch center where they can use their bodies while adding and subtracting the numbers that appear on a roll of dice (see Figure 8.2). Or in an ABC center, groups of children might use their bodies to make letters, photograph them, and add them to an alphabet book. The key is to imagine ways for these children—as much as possible—to engage their whole bodies as they play and learn.

Figure 1.6. Friends reading together in the reading nook

Interpersonal Intelligence

Children with high interpersonal intelligence are keenly sensitive to the feelings of others and they often recognize when another child is sad and offer comfort. These children enjoy playing in ways that allow them to interact thoughtfully with their classmates—for example, small-group center activities, particularly reading with friends in the reading nook (see Figure 1.6) or working on a group project at the art table. In dramatic play, these children often take on the roles of caregivers. Interpersonal intelligence is required for a class to feel like a community, so it's important to support its development in all children, even those who don't exhibit it in obvious ways. Talking with children about how to recognize another's feelings is a good first step toward helping children use their interpersonal intelligence to guide their play more effectively.

Intrapersonal Intelligence

Children with high intrapersonal intelligence have self-confidence and are able to express their feelings and ask for specific help with assignments. These children find inspiration in the more challenging centers, particularly when the activities are extensions of class studies. The key to supporting intrapersonal intelligence is observing children at play and figuring out ways to use their interests to suggest new and exciting challenges.

Naturalistic Intelligence

Children with high naturalistic intelligence are very aware of the environment; these are the children who can identify every subway line in New York City or who remember that you have to pass three bodegas on the way to the park. They see patterns in the environment and are interested in how objects, people, and animals interact. A good sense of direction comes from naturalistic intelligence, and children who are strong in this area may be challenged by a map-making activity or by making a guide to the school or a familiar place. If the dramatic play center needs to be redesigned to represent a class investigation (as a firehouse or market or barbershop, for example), children with naturalistic intelligence will have an eye for detail that will lend authenticity to the space. Any play that can happen outdoors and involves children noticing and exploring the environment will support children's naturalistic intelligence.

Existential Intelligence

Children with existential intelligence think big thoughts and ask challenging questions about life and existence: *How did the stars get into the sky? Why don't they fall on us? Do you think that someday people will be able to live forever?* The kinds of questions these children ask can't always be answered, but they can be explored and the key is to support these explorations. To encourage these children, consider setting up a research center (see children

Figure 1.7 Firehouse research

doing research about the firehouse in Figure 1.7) where children can use the Internet and nonfiction books to find out and record information related to their questions (or a class study). An observation center where children watch the sky or animals or people can support existential thinking. In a survey center, these children might be drawn to composing abstract, higher-order questions. And because big questions can occur at any time, consider creating a "wonder wall" or some other space where children can go on their own to record a big question.

If we expect children to think creatively and make interesting connections to the curriculum, we need to recognize and respect children who, like adults, have many ways of interacting, discovering, remembering, and learning. With thoughtful planning, you can create choice time activities that will appeal to the many kinds of learners in a classroom.

Multiple intelligences can be a useful lens through which you observe children. As you collect notes on students across the year, consider reviewing them from time to time with this lens in mind. What picture of each child emerges when you consider what you've observed over time? Do the child's choices, actions, and interactions suggest a dominant intelligence? Are there ways you might support each child even more intentionally to explore the world from a position of strength?

Planning with Student Interests in Mind

Before a new group of students ever arrives at school, we use our understanding of different kinds of play and different intelligences to set up the classroom and establish enriching centers for children to explore. This preplanning serves many purposes:

- It is multilayered.
- It provides a framework and vision for how each center will be organized.
- It allows us to be ready with the necessary tools and materials.
- It gives us the clarity and confidence we need to explain the educational learning that will take place at each center to parents, peers, and administrators.

As soon as the children walk through the door, however, a different sort of planning begins, and it's all based on these *particular* children who have experiences and interests all their own. No two groups of children are exactly the same, of course, and any particular group will be different two months from now than it is at this moment. So in addition to learning styles, it's also incredibly important to consider children's interests as centers and choices evolve over time. This is why planning for centers is based on careful observation and is ongoing, fluid, and responsive.

After we've organized and introduced centers, we carefully observe how children are using the centers and also which children are attracted to which centers (and which they avoid). We listen carefully. What are children talking about? Is there a particular interest children have that we might incorporate more strategically into their center activities? If we see, for example, that a group of children has a keen interest in vehicles but shies away from the art center, we might shift the focus of the art center to constructing different vehicles. We could plan a class minilesson to brainstorm different types of cars and trucks students could build and then invite the vehicle builders to draw up plans for their creations using graph paper, pencils, rulers, and books and pictures for research. We would observe again, studying how their work was evolving, and then we'd plan next steps. Do we need more minilessons? A shelf to display what children have created? Will we invite children to write about their vehicles or draw and label diagrams?

Over time, planning for centers must also be responsive to the interests of the class as a whole. For example, if a classwide study of the neighborhood has taken a particular turn to an interest in bridges, then center activities might be directed toward that interest. We might

- add books and photos of bridges to the block center and art center;
- provide art materials that lend themselves to bridge construction, such as cardboard strips, string, and yarn;
- challenge children in the math center to use manipulatives (triangles, squares, rectangles) to build a bridge; or
- add books about bridges to the reading nook.

We can also connect center activities to reading workshop. If we are studying folktales, we can provide pigs and a copy of *The Three Little Pigs* in the block center as an incentive for children to re-create the story. Usually just a few small props are enough to inspire children to make connections without having been explicitly told to do so.

As we observe and interact with children in centers, our minds are always on both the present and the future. We are thinking carefully about what's happening and also making plans for how best to extend the center work to support children's growth and development. This in-the-moment planning keeps us focused very specifically on the particular strengths and interests of a group of children, and it ensures we offer the focus and clarity children need to support their explorations.

Communicating with Families

All parents and caregivers want their children to succeed. People may differ in their definitions of success, but nobody wishes a child to be unhappy and unsuccessful. Some families and caregivers instinctively understand the benefits of inquiry, play, and choice. Others may be afraid that choice activities take time away from important academic lessons. It's our responsibility to open positive lines of communication with families, keeping them abreast of the learning that is taking place in our classrooms.

Some families enjoy receiving weekly or monthly newsletters describing what is going on in their child's classroom. To convey the importance of the work children accomplish during choice time, we need to prioritize it and be specific about the explorations taking place. We might highlight one or two activities in each newsletter, describing the play that takes place and how reading, writing, and math are integrated. If children are exploring magnets at the science center, we could include a recording sheet on which a child has documented what a magnet will and will not hold, a few notes from our observations, and a transcript of children having a conversation about this phenomenon.

Sending home a weekly calendar at the start of each month worked best for me (see Figure 1.8 on the next page). Besides showing the flow of each day, I included the title of the chapter book I was reading, the focus of our reading, writing, and mathematics work, our social studies and science projects, and also some of the highlights for choice time. Parents came to expect this and complained if it arrived late! They were able to glance at the schedule to see what their child was doing each day and use this information to engage their child in talk about school. Of course I let parents know that this schedule was more like a road map of our week and not a timetable that I kept to with a stopwatch. What was most important was that parents viewed me as a partner. We, too, need to consider parents our partners and allies in our yearlong voyage together. After all, they are trusting us with their most important treasures!

Fall	Kindergarten 2-239							Renée Dinnerstein and Rohini Thakor	
Mon.	8:35 Settling in and Independent Reading	9:00 Morning Meeting	9:20 Bridge Study and Choice Time	10:55 Music Ms. Gbaje	11:40 Lunch	12:00 Shared Reading and Reading Workshop	1:00 Outdoor Play	1:45 Writing Workshop	2:40 Read-Aloud and Singing
Tues.	8:35 Settling in and Independent Reading	9:00 Morning Meeting	9:20 Choice Time	10:20 Math	11:00 Outdoor Play	11:40 Lunch	12:30 Shared Reading and Reading Workshop	1:10 Writing Workshop	2:00 Read-Aloud / 2:15 Body Movement Ms. Sachs
Wed.	8:40 Science (Ms. Bell) Room 102	9:35 Morning Meeting	9:50 Bridge Study and Choice Time	11:00 Shared Reading and Reading Workshop	11:40 Lunch	12:30 Math Games	1:00 Outdoor Play	1:40 Read-Aloud	2:00 Reading with Fourth-Grade Buddies (Bridge Books)
Thurs.	8:35 Settling in and Independent Reading	9:00 Morning Meeting	9:20 Choice Time	10:20 Math	11:10 Read-Aloud	11:40 Lunch	12:30 Outdoor Play	1:15 Writing Workshop	2:15 Shared Reading/Reading Workshop (Every third week/ grade meeting)
Fri.	8:35 Settling in and Independent Reading	9:00 Morning Meeting	9:15 Social Studies and Choice Time	10:10 Gym Mr. Polsky	10:55 Music Mr. McGarry	11:40 Lunch	12:30 Shared Reading and Reading Workshop	1:00 Outdoor Play	1:40 Project Research Groups / 2:25 Read-Aloud and Singing

Science Focus at Choice Time Science Center: Snails

Social Studies Inquiry Investigation: Bridges (working with our fourth-grade buddies on this investigation)

At "research groups," (Reading Centers) children are preparing for a class "camping trip" (inspired by a Berenstain Bears book that Lee shared with the class). The reading groups, based on children's suggestions, are Trees, Flowers, Forest Animals, Goldilocks and the Three Bears, Little Red Riding Hood, Rocks, Stars. Coming out of this research are ideas for choice time projects.

For read-aloud, I am reading Ramona the Pest.

Figure 1.8. Using the class schedule to communicate with families

2

The Classroom Speaks

In the opening segment of the wonderful children's show *Mister Rogers' Neighborhood*, Fred Rogers welcomes his young viewers into the neighborhood, singing about the beautiful day and inviting them to be his special neighbors. Monday through Friday, for nearly ten months each school year, the classroom is the neighborhood we share with our students. And just as Mr. Rogers created a safe and welcoming neighborhood for his friends (Daniel Striped Tiger, Lady Aberlin, Mr. McFeely), we work hard to create a gentle, exciting space of our own. Ideally, it's a laboratory for exploratory learning, a place where children build things, conduct experiments, create innovative art projects, read fascinating books, write original stories, use technology and texts to find out information, and feel free to imagine and try out possibilities. It's a place where children grow big ideas, make new friends, and dig deeply into exciting investigations.

When children and their families first walk into a classroom at the beginning of a new school year, what they see all around them tells them a lot about the neighborhood they will inhabit. Each classroom has a voice, and the position of the furniture, the materials, what's on the walls—everything, really—*speak* and tell the children whom and what you value. The voice is so powerful, in fact, that teachers in the schools in Reggio Emilia say the classroom is the second teacher. They design their classrooms to encourage children's independence and provide space for collaboration and creative thinking. Visiting the early childhood and elementary classrooms in Reggio Emilia, one is immediately impressed by the clarity of organization, lack of clutter, and aesthetic beauty of the spaces filled with plants and other natural artifacts. Children can access materials without adult assistance. There is a palpable sense of co-ownership.

A Room with a Voice

Every summer, rooms piled with cartons, chairs, and tables await the transformation that takes place when the children return to inhabit and animate the space. This image of a classroom with a voice guides our decisions about arranging the furniture and selecting the materials that will be waiting for the children on their first day of school. Even the simplest decisions can speak volumes. A terrarium placed at the eye level of a six-year-old, for example, says something very different than a terrarium placed out of reach on top of a bookshelf. When a classroom speaks, the message is obvious to all who pass through its doors. A classroom can say to each child:

- I welcome you to this exciting, caring place.
- You are now part of a community that works, plays, and shares together.
- You are a very special, important member of this community.
- In this room, you will be an explorer, a creator, and a scientist.
- You will find many ways to record and share your discoveries.

- You are a literate person who can already read and write. (Even the youngest child can re-create a story by reading the illustrations and can make marks on paper that are meaningful to that child.) Together we will learn more about reading and writing.
- Because we are a sharing community, there will be times when we all come together as a group.
- Because you are a unique individual, there will be times when you will have a private place to be alone with your thoughts.
- Because we value and seek out one another's ideas, we will have time and places to meet in small groups.
- We are a community that always shows respect and compassion for one another and for all living things.
- We will celebrate one another's achievements.

The challenge for us as teachers is not so much in deciding *what* we want our classrooms to say but in knowing *how* to say it.

> Take a few moments to observe your classroom closely. Look at the layout of furniture, the materials, what's hanging on the walls. What does the room say about what you value and the learning life you share with your students? You might invite your students to consider the same question. Ask, "If our classroom could speak, what would it say about us?"

Most of us start thinking about organizing our classrooms during the summer, well before the school doors open. All during August, we draw sketchy diagrams of possible classroom arrangements. Thinking ahead about room arrangement, of course, goes hand in hand with thinking about curriculum. As we consider what we will be teaching, particularly at the start of the year, we also envision what materials we'll need and where different activities will take place. We think about where we will be meeting as a class, where we will work with small groups, and where children will be doing their own small-group and whole-group work. We think about how much independence we want children to have. Will we have all the centers set up and ready on the first day, or will the

Figure 2.1. Bill Fulbrecht contemplates the space as he sets up his room in August.

children help set them up once they arrive? And what about the daily schedule? Once everything is set up, how will each day flow?

So many decisions to make as we arrange and rearrange and rearrange until the children finally arrive and the space comes to life and we rearrange all over again based on how they move around the room. Designing a classroom layout that works for us and our students can seem like a daunting task. How do we make decisions about space, materials, displays, and time that say clearly to our students, "Welcome to our neighborhood. It's your special place. I'm so glad you've come"?

Space

When space in a classroom speaks, the arrangement of furniture and materials tells a lot about how the community lives and works together. Children see wide-open spaces and cozy corners and everything in between, and they imagine different ways of being in all the different spaces. While we don't have any control over the actual dimensions of our classroom space, there are all kinds of decisions we can make that will impact how much space we'll have inside those dimensions and how we'll use it.

Furniture

A certain amount of furniture in a classroom is a necessity, but it's important to think about both what you have and what you need when it comes to the layout of furniture in the room. First, carefully consider every single furnishing and whether it is essential or not. For example, do you really need that big desk, or would a file cabinet and a small shelf suffice? How much space would it save if you did get rid of it? How else might you use that space? For a center, perhaps? Consider removing any piece of furniture that's not essential and also favoring any piece that can do double or triple duty during the day. A toy chest, for example, might hold dramatic play props and also function as a table.

Another important furniture consideration is size. You need tables and chairs and shelves that are a good match for children's bodies, of course, but it's also important that furniture not block your vision of a classroom full of busy children. Shelves and file cabinets do great triple duty as material storage, display space, and room dividers, but if you can't see over them easily, they're a problem. If this is an issue, see if you might swap high bookcases and cabinets for low ones with other teachers in the building. Ideally, the landscape of a classroom where young children work and play has a low profile.

Layout

As you consider the arrangement of furniture and materials in the room, think of the classroom as a laboratory for exploration. Instead of positioning all the tables in the center of the room, isolating them from investigation centers, divide the room into discrete areas, ready for children's explorations (see Figures 2.2, 2.3, and 2.4).

Consider the kinds of spaces you will need across the day. Most classrooms have at least one meeting space that is big enough for all the children in the room to gather together. Since this space will take up the greatest square footage, it's important to think about where it will be located. The meeting area should not be too close to the classroom door. If it is, meetings will be interrupted anytime someone enters or leaves the room.

When the whole class is not together, the meeting area can be used for other purposes. Since it's big and open, it might be used for centers that involve a lot of movement and action. As long as the materials for the center are stored in transportable containers, the space can be transformed quickly. It's not a space where children can leave materials from day to day, however, so any center requiring ongoing activity won't work as well here. The meeting area could also be used at the same time by multiple small groups and even for center activities that don't require tables or a lot of space. Children can read independently in the meeting area during reading workshop, and with lap boards, they might

Figure 2.2. One second-grade classroom layout

Figure 2.3. Large tables placed as close to centers as possible

Figure 2.4. This teacher arranged her tables around a center island.

also use the space for writing. If the space is defined by bookshelves, it can double as the classroom library.

Outside the meeting area, it's important to decide whether you are going to have any other dedicated areas in the room such as a block center, a reading nook, or a writing table by the window. There are several benefits to having dedicated spaces in the room. For one, if you know that children are likely to be noisy when using the space, you can make sure it's separated from places where children need quiet. If you create a dedicated space away from the flow of traffic, children will have plenty of room for building and moving around their constructions without fear of unintended mishaps. You can equip and outfit a dedicated space with all sorts of supports for the designated activity, and you can base the size and location of the space on the nature of the activity itself.

Ideally, a classroom would have dedicated areas for all its permanent centers, but whether or not that's possible really depends on how much space you have. You have to look at how big (or small) your space is and then think about how you can use it most efficiently. What trade-offs can you make? For example, if you're longing for a spacious block center, you might do away with the dramatic play center and store the materials and hollow blocks on a shelf by the meeting area. Again, practically any space can do double duty during the day as long as materials are easy to store and transport.

In addition to the meeting area and any dedicated center space you want to create, you also have to think about space for all the centers you will have up and running on any given day. How many centers you have really depends on how many students you have, how much space, and sometimes how many adults are in the room. There need to be enough centers for children to feel as if they truly have a choice about where they will go. This doesn't mean, of course, that they will always get their *first* choice (because they are part of a group of children making choices); it just means they can be confident that there are interesting choices available to them.

Once you have a number of centers in mind (based on the number of children you have), then it's time to look around the room and figure out where each of those centers might take place. How much room will children need? Children in an art center, for example, will need space for big collaborative projects with lots of materials, while children in a science or math center might work on a tabletop with all the tools and materials they need for their explorations neatly organized and stored. Remember that any tables you use for explorations during center time can also be used during whole-class activities such as writing workshop and math lessons. Also consider the noise and activity levels of each center and try to separate them accordingly.

Finally, once you've figured out where all the centers are going to be, it's important to consider the flow of traffic around the room. Can children move easily from place to place? If not, can you relocate any of the centers, or might you need to streamline the number of centers to fit the space? Are materials located strategically to prevent overcrowding? Traffic flow can be tricky to predict because certain groups of children simply move through space differently than others. A space that worked perfectly the year before might for some reason create a major issue for this year's class. In the first days and weeks of school, you'll want to observe the movement in your classroom during center time and make adjustments based on how you see students using the space.

Materials

A primary classroom is filled with materials: a pair of binoculars by a window, a plastic jar full of colorful buttons, a basket of books about dinosaurs. When materials in a classroom speak, they tell about whom children can be in that center—readers, writers, mathematicians, musicians, artists, explorers, actors, builders. The possibilities are endless. Materials also speak of access, of course, and children can see immediately how easily they can (or can't) get their hands on things.

While each of the chapters that follow considers the kinds of materials that make sense for different centers, here we just want to think about storage and access. You will have to decide how much independence you want children to have. When spaces and centers are clearly delineated, children can access materials easily, and the careful organization of each center helps students use the materials purposefully in their investigations and play. It's probably best not to put out a lot of materials at the beginning of the year. You can add them slowly as children learn how to care for the centers and seem ready to extend their explorations. Over time, the more independence children have, the more likely they are to feel ownership of the classroom community.

As you consider where all your different materials will be stored, be sure to leave plenty of open spaces on tops of shelves or other surfaces where children can store and display their work in progress (see Figure 2.5). Children need to be able to return to their center projects and expand them from day to day, and having this space encourages them to work on projects for an extended period of time. If they feel a personal engagement and are given time and space to do so, children will do this just as they continue working on a piece in writing workshop or reading a book in reading workshop.

Displays

What we see on display when we enter a classroom, even when there are no children present, tells us so much about its life. A classroom where students are learning about bridges is filled with paintings, models, drawings, and photographs of bridges, and children's bridge poems and stories are on display in the classroom library, ready to be read. Shelves in a classroom in which students are exploring recycled materials display sculptures created with pieces of wood, buttons, wires, and other found materials; next to them are children's drawings and stories about these creations. When displays speak, they tell the story of learning that is unfolding inside the classroom. (See Figure 2.6.)

Figure 2.5. These shelves display both finished work and work in progress.

Figure 2.6. This shelf offers second graders an invitation to create.

Displays can also speak to children and let them know how much they are valued. Commercial wall charts are mass-produced by people who have no connection to our students, so it's very difficult for children to see their lives reflected in these displays. Rather than decorating the walls with premade number charts, color charts, or charts listing class rules, consider having students participate in creating these charts. When children decide what image best represents *A* in their minds, or how to picture the number four, the chart becomes so much more meaningful. Collaboratively created charts listing strategies for writing stories, cleanup routines, or ideas for a class investigation make teaching and learning visible for children and teachers (Mraz and Martinelli 2014). Jean McPadden, a former kindergarten teacher at PS 321 in Brooklyn, refers to the many charts strung up across classrooms as literacy laundry! Once the charts are no longer being referenced by you or the children, it's time to retire them until they're relevant again.

In addition to the charts that support and document learning, displays of children's work in a classroom speak loudly and clearly about what you value. When you display children's paintings and sculptures and other artwork, it shows an appreciation for their aesthetic sensibilities. Photos of children at work and play serve the same purpose they do in people's homes: they say, "You *live* here. This is your space." When we display children's writing as children composed it (not "corrected" by an adult), we send the message that we value approximations because it's OK to be learning. When we show off children's quirky inventions that may not work so well but were great ideas, we show how much we value the imaginative process. Finally, when we display the creations children choose to make during their center time explorations, we show that we value their independent work as much as—if not more than—the work they do because we've asked them to do it. After all, a room filled with all sorts of unique student work has a whole different feel to it than a room displaying twenty-five identical art projects or twenty-five stories written with the exact same sentence starter.

Time

It may be that of all the voices in the classroom, time actually speaks the loudest. How we use time during the day speaks volumes about our beliefs about teaching and learning and our understanding of the developmental needs of young children. Just as the heart pumps blood through the blood vessels of the circulatory system, providing the body with oxygen and important nutrients, choice activities are vital to the well-being of young children and to their intellectual, social, and emotional growth. Centers create energy, excitement, and enthusiasm that weave their way through the school day (Venes 2009).

In his book *Yardsticks* (1996), Chip Wood describes developmental characteristics for children between the ages of four and fourteen. He notes the following about students in preK through second grade:

- Four-year-olds are interested in manipulative experiences ("magnets, pulleys in science, puzzles . . . scoops, funnels, measuring cups" [36]) and they love to work in groups and engage in parallel play. They are also ready to learn rules and social skills.

- Five-year-olds learn best through play.

- Six-year-olds like new games, experimenting with new ideas, engaging in elaborate dramatic play, using new skills and techniques, and having "an artistic explosion—clay, paints, dancing" (64). They are discoverers who enjoy working on big projects.

- Seven-year-olds need to make things perfect, are not as process oriented, and are more interested in the finished product. They are "driven by curiosity and a strong internal desire to discover and invent" (72) and enjoy working with a partner.

At various carefully prepared centers, we scaffold children's natural instinct for play, introducing materials and posing questions and ideas that help them develop a wide range of skills. Children have the opportunity to set their own agendas and cocreate the rules and scenarios intrinsic to play and investigation (Wood 1996). They particularly enjoy building with unit blocks, playing with sand and water and having other science experiences at a science center, working with manipulatives at the math center, acting out real-life scenarios in the dramatic play center, sharing favorite storybooks with friends in a cozy reading nook, and experimenting with paint and other creative materials in the art center.

Scheduling Time for Choice—Prekindergarten and Kindergarten

Because choice activities are such an important part of the preschool and kindergarten curriculum, whenever possible, they should take place during prime instructional time, and the earlier in the day, the better. When children participate in center activities at the end of the day, their play is understandably less focused on collaborative interactions and creative explorations. They're tired from their academic work and less interested in writing a story or recording magnet discoveries or creating menus for a restaurant. By the end of a day without opportunities for playful, freely chosen experiences, children often treat center activities as unguided free play—and who can blame them? Children certainly need time every day to set their own play agenda without adult intervention (on the school playground, for example), but choice activities have a different purpose. Because we plan our centers so carefully and take the play children engage in seriously, centers should not be considered a coda at the end of the school day or a reward for good behavior.

In my experience, the best time for children to focus on choice activities is between morning meeting and reading workshop. At the end of morning meeting, during which I may have introduced new center materials, a new strategy for using center materials, or a new center, students make their choices and then head off to their chosen areas. (Strategies for helping children choose centers are discussed in Chapter 3.) The period always ends with a brief, focused sharing session, followed by singing some of our favorite songs—a joyous way of getting ready for the next part of our day.

Sometimes, of course, factors beyond our control influence our scheduling decisions and it's just not possible to have choice time when we'd most like to have it. When this is the case, the hour just before lunch or following an after-lunch read-aloud is a good alternative. The bottom line is, if we believe that the explorations children do in centers are vital to their development, we make the best decision we possibly can to give them prime instructional time for their center activities.

Scheduling Time for Choice—First and Second Grades

In first and second grade, children are developmentally more mature and there are new curricular demands. Integrating choice activities into a day filled with academic subjects, along with the arts and physical education, is more challenging, but it's not impossible. Many first- and second-grade teachers use center time to focus on opportunities for children to explore materials that extend and elaborate the academic curriculum. Instead of calling this part of the choice time, it is often referred to as *inquiry centers* since they are so closely connected to classroom inquiry projects. For example, first graders who are learning about life cycles in science might extend their understanding of metamorphosis as they observe and record mealworms changing to beetles in the science center. Second graders who are analyzing shapes in their math lessons might explore the symmetry, volume, and area of these shapes in the math center.

First-grade New York City public school teacher Alexis McClelland and her students were studying the city's subway system. Her choice activities—about an hour, two times a week, during a part of the day when children were alert and eager to participate in collaborative activities—gave children the opportunity to dig deeper into this inquiry. Students could choose among the following activities:

- comparing subway maps from different cities and creating a subway map, with a key for stations and routes, for students' own imaginary city
- polling classmates about subway ridership, creating a graph summarizing the responses, and sharing this information with the class
- designing subway car models using photographs and sketches
- using subway sounds to create musical compositions
- writing and illustrating poems that could be displayed on a subway car billboard

- painting a subway mural
- constructing subway cars out of blocks
- using an interactive whiteboard to research subway routes to various city landmarks (the Empire State Building, for example) and plot class trips, as well as drawing illustrations of the landmarks
- creating a subway station in the dramatic play area (with a turnstile, signs, seats, payment cards, and so on).

Facing a second-grade curriculum packed with math, science, reading, writing, word study, and social studies, another New York City teacher, Rachel Schwartzman, thought carefully about how and when children would get the opportunity to participate in center activities. She decided to use them to extend her students' study of city architecture, and since her class had a late lunch period, she set aside one afternoon a week for children to work on their projects.

Figure 2.7. A second-grade collaborative building project

After visiting various landmark buildings in the city, each student designed her or his own building. Then small groups of students (see Figure 2.7) chose one design they would construct out of materials available in the classroom. Collaborative work included discussing which design to use. Some groups combined elements from various drawings into a compilation that pleased everyone; others chose one drawing from the group. The students then used straws, aluminum foil, toothpicks, clay, and various other materials (one group used wooden blocks; another used Legos) to construct their buildings.

With these various choice activities, Alexis and Rachel were able to support their students' developmental need to collaborate, play, and explore and also deepen their understandings of curriculum in significant ways.

A classroom "speaks" to the powerful conditions for learning identified by Brian Cambourne (1988):

- *Immersion:* When centers are filled with carefully chosen materials, children are immersed in possibilities for exploring and creating.

- *Demonstration:* In whole-class minilessons and in interactions while children are in centers, the teacher demonstrates the many possibilities for discovery and exploration.

- *Expectation:* The teacher communicates high expectations and respect for center explorations each time he or she asks children to share what they have done in centers.

- *Responsibility:* Children are totally responsible for how they use the tools and materials in each center, and the possibilities are as endless as their imagination and interests.

- *Practice:* In centers, children are not rushed and they have time to practice newly acquired skills and to experiment with unfamiliar materials over and over again (especially when they return to centers that interest them).

- *Approximation:* Children are free to experiment and approximate during center time and come up with their own solutions to the problems they encounter.

- *Response:* In a classroom filled with centers, response is abundant because the teacher interacts with children constantly—asking questions, naming actions, and giving feedback.

- *Engagement:* From start to finish, center time is designed to support children's engagement as they make decisions and guide their own exploration and play.

3

A Classroom Where Centers Thrive

In a kindergarten class, *Jesse and Lila are playing in the art center, putting the finishing touches on their playground for the snails that live in the science center. Lila is placing some tape on the structure when Jesse suggests, "Put the yogurt cup here so if they fall, they'll fall here." Lila agrees and suggests they should make it soft, so Jesse looks over the selection of materials in the art center and picks up a piece of bubble paper. "This is soft," he says.*

Jesse stuffs the yogurt cup with bubble paper and then moves the cup under a string that they taped across the box. "This is if they fall. We can catch them."

Lila moves the cup to the corner of the box and explains the move will give them more space if they aren't climbing up high. She crosses two Popsicle sticks together and tapes them. "Here's a climbing tree. The snails will like them."

Watching children like Lila and Jesse engaged so thoughtfully in their play (see Figure 3.1) makes us long for school days where there could be "so much time and so little to do." But of course, as Dahl points out in *Charlie and the Great Glass Elevator* (1972), this is the exact reverse of our real dilemma. "How can I fit it all in?" is the question we face each year. What if we reframed the dilemma: "How can I find the time for a vigorous and challenging curriculum without racing children through the school day?" By posing the question this way, we name the *it*—a vigorous and challenging curriculum—and are able to see its significance more clearly in relation to time. In "Statements of Beliefs About Children,"

Figure 3.1. Constructing a playground for the snails

the editors of *The Teacher You Want to Be* assert clearly, "We believe children need time, both within a school day and across a school year, to deeply explore topics of importance and interest" (Glover and Keene 2015, 234). Understanding this as something children *need* for their development makes it much more than just another thing to fit into a busy day.

Time

As you think about where choice time will fit into your schedule, a practical approach is to make a blank template for each day of the week. Begin by filling in the nonnegotiable periods (e.g., lunch, recess, clusters, art, gym). Next, block out periods for literacy and math instruction. You'll need time for read-aloud, reading workshop (which might include shared and guided reading), writing workshop, word study, and mathematics. If there are any specific enrichments, add those next. For example, in some schools, each grade might have a one-semester dance or puppetry enrichment.

Once everything that is required is on the schedule, it's time to think about the ages of your students and how much time you'll need for choice time. Regardless of the grade you teach, you'll want to find as much time as you possibly can, but most importantly, you have to consider the developmental needs of your students. Prekindergarten children might have periods for play-based activities twice daily, whereas second graders could have inquiry centers once or twice a week.

When you have a sense of how much time you're looking for, it's time for some creative maneuvering. One option you might consider is to integrate social studies and science into your centers. If you follow content area lessons with choice time, you can plan centers that build on these lessons. In second grade, you might consider dedicating one afternoon a week to inquiry center work, connecting it to your social studies and science projects.

Another possibility is to experiment with breaking up the literacy block across the day. Choice time might follow a period of morning reading, and then the children could move into writing workshop. When kindergarten and first-grade children have choice time in the morning or right after lunch, they are better able to focus on a more formal activity such as writing or math afterward.

If you have full periods set aside for enrichments, you might try folding these extras into choice time centers. I was able to do this with the Studio in a School program. Instead of spending an entire period once a week with the whole class, the artist did a short demonstration lesson at our meeting before center time, introducing a particular technique or new material to everyone. A group of children would then work in the art center with the artist as I observed and took notes and photographs. I continued the center for the rest of the week so all the children had an opportunity to try out the new techniques or materials in the art center.

Predictable Routines

Predictable routines for choice time make planning easier and eliminate the anxiety of not knowing what is happening next for children. Of course, you will always leave room for flexibility and the joy of serendipity; however, improvisation will be most successful within a framework of predictability (Cazden 2001).

A workshop model provides the necessary structure and routine for centers. Each choice time begins with the children gathered in the meeting area for a brief teacher-led minilesson that connects to some aspect of that day's choice time. After the lesson, you might read and discuss the choices that are posted on a chart and give each child an opportunity to select a choice. After selecting an activity, each child goes to his or her chosen center for a period of independent play—the "meat" of choice time. In centers around the room, children explore, play, and investigate. During this time, you might be facilitating one particular center (such as a cooking activity) or moving about the room, observing and offering children stimulating and provocative feedback.

After a signal that there are five minutes remaining, children begin cleaning up their centers. Choice time ends when the class gathers together for a share meeting. The share meeting gives children opportunities to consider what they played, achieved, or discovered during choice time. It's an opportunity to support children in learning to listen carefully, ask pertinent questions, and keep a line of questioning moving forward. Sharing will often circle back to the focus of the minilesson. Reflection journals also give children an opportunity to record and share something about their experiences in choice time centers (see Figure 3.2).

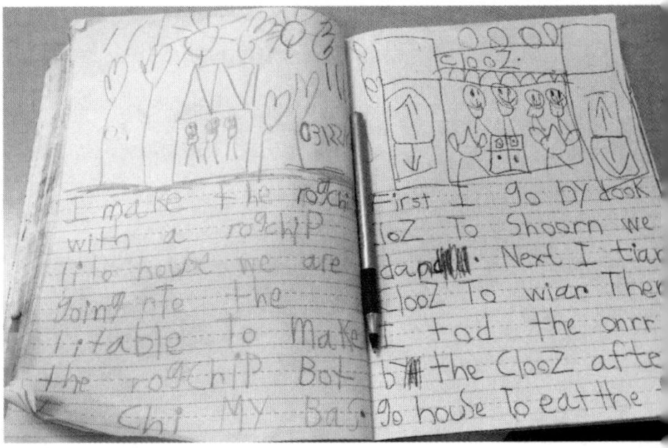

Figure 3.2. An ELL kindergartner writes about an experience at the light table center one day and at dramatic play the next.

Whole-Class Lessons

The focus of the minilessons in choice time will often come from your observations and relate directly to the needs of the children. For example, if you notice children not interacting at centers, you might prepare a series of lessons over a few days focused on strategies or examples of how children might work together. Here are some other possibilities for organization and procedure lessons that offer children strategies for choice time. You might talk with children about

- routines of the workshop structure: minilesson, independent explorations, and the share meeting;
- considerations for choosing centers;
- planning with peers for how to work on a project in a center;
- procedures for cleaning different centers;
- what to do after a center is cleaned up; or
- recording reflections in a post–choice time journal.

If a new center is opening, the minilesson might introduce the center, and then on consecutive days, the children might brainstorm ideas for what they could do with the materials in that center. For example, Katie Rust's first-grade class was investigating how cars helped move people about the city. They had many opportunities to observe cars in the street, visit a garage and interview the mechanic, investigate the inside of a stretch limousine, visit parking garages, and study the meters in their neighborhood. One day Katie came to school with a large, rectangular piece of Styrofoam. For her minilesson, she shared the Styrofoam and invited the children to discuss possibilities for using it in their centers. A group of children decided to use it to construct a car. They took some suggestions from the class on materials to use and committed to drawing up a design plan for their construction (see Figure 3.3). A new center began!

Figure 3.3. Making the car

Here are some other possibilities for minilessons that introduce a new center with unfamiliar materials:

- adding a new type of paper to the art center
- turning the dramatic play area into a restaurant
- setting up a snail habitat in the science center
- working with a variety of measuring tools in the block center
- including adding machine tape with the math materials

Choices

Because children will need to choose a center each day, it's important that you establish an efficient routine for making selections. First, children need to be able to survey all their choices. A choice chart that is clear and easy for children to read displays all the center choices available, and you can add each new center to the chart as you introduce it. For the youngest children, pictures should illustrate each choice on the chart (see Figure 3.4).

Review how many children may go to each center. You might ask children to consider how many could play well

Figure 3.4. Making choices at the chart

together at each center and let them make that decision. If their ideas don't work out agreeably, that will create an opportunity for a meaningful discussion at the share meeting.

Next, establish a predictable routine for selection. In my classroom, I listed the children's names on a chart and moved a clip down the chart from one name to the next each day. The child whose name was by the clip had first choice, and the child who had first choice the previous day had last choice (see Figure 3.5). I also made it clear that children who were in the middle of a project could stay at their center for as many days as it took to complete it.

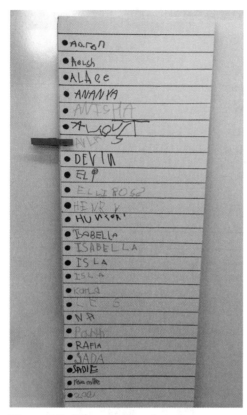

Figure 3.5. Who goes next?

If you encourage children to think of more than one choice that appeals to them, it helps them choose more quickly and without anxiety if their first preference is "closed." Assure children that if they don't get their first choice, the center will remain open and available for as long as they have interest (be sure to follow up on this promise).

Finally, there should be more opportunities for centers to play in than there are children in the class. It's important that children truly have opportunities for making choices and that they are not stuck with whatever center is left when it's their time to choose.

Cleanup Time

My mother often repeated the mantra, "A place for everything and everything in its place," in her attempt to help her three daughters, who shared one bedroom, keep our room orderly and respect each other's property. I often remembered those words when I tried to help my students assume a shared responsibility for the upkeep of their classroom centers. Cleaning up is an important part of learning independence and responsibility.

Even when we have spent lots of time helping children learn good cleanup strategies, there are times when everything seems to fall apart and chaos reigns. Connie Norgren was a teacher who was about to give up on choice time because of the mess it created each day. Instead, she decided to turn cleanup into an inquiry itself.

Connie introduced her plan before choice time one morning with a class discussion about the noise and chaos of cleanup time. It became evident that the children did not have a clear understanding of their responsibilities, and they were also uncertain about what they should be doing after their center was put in order. Connie suggested the children help her develop a chart with a clear, step-by-step plan for cleaning up their centers and getting ready for the next class activity.

When the children came to school the next day, the chart was posted on the easel in the meeting area and each child also had a copy on his or her own clipboard (see Figure 3.6). Connie explained that each day that week she would stop choice time earlier than usual and they would all get their clipboards. As they did each cleanup task, they would check it off on their personal charts. At the share meeting, they could discuss how the plan was working.

Figure 3.6. Connie's cleanup chart

The children were excited to get started, and when Connie announced cleanup, they eagerly checked off each step on their charts. After a week of shorter center times and longer cleanup sessions, they had another meeting to reflect on how this experiment worked. The children agreed that the charts could be put away because, as Connie told them, they were now wonderfully responsible cleanup helpers!

Periodically, over the next few months, the class read the chart to review the routines. By giving the children the opportunity to work together on creating a workable cleanup plan, Connie helped them have a better understanding of the value of collaboration and responsibility.

At the beginning of the year, explicitly model how to clean up each center area and give children time to practice and articulate the cleanup routines. Decide whether children will have cleanup jobs or whether each group will clean up their own center. You might want to follow Connie's example and create a "How We Clean Up" chart together with the children. This is most effective when it's done after children have experienced a few cleanup sessions and reflected on the routines. The book *Smarter Charts*, by Marjorie Martinelli and Kristie Mraz (2014), has many helpful suggestions for creating charts with children.

Most teachers have some sort of signal that tells children it's time to begin cleaning up. Some use a small bell or chimes, while others sing a cleanup song. My class particularly liked the Woody Guthrie song "Pick It Up." I suggest you avoiding flickering the lights, as that can distress many children and cause hyperactivity. Finally, make sure children understand where to go and what to do when they have finished cleaning up. Will they help other children in their centers? Will they come to the rug and take a book? May they have quiet conversations with friends?

Reflections and Plans

When you are clear about your goals for each center, you can use that clarity as a lens through which to reflect on children's activities. You might begin by asking yourself a few leading questions, such as these:

- Are my centers organized in a way that invites children to work with increasing independence?
- Is there enough physical space for children to work on their chosen projects?
- Is it clear to children where they can find materials?
- Do children understand that materials are fluid and can be moved from one center to another if they need them?
- Are there sufficient—but not too many—materials in the center to engage children over time?

The simple template in Figure 3.7 is a helpful tool for reflecting and for planning the ongoing activities in centers. See Appendix A for the full-size reproducible.

Frequently Asked Questions

Any teacher who is considering adding choice time to the schedule for the first time will no doubt have lots of questions. And while the questions are common, there are no simple answers to most of them. Teachers who are working in the moment do, at times, need to improvise, and this is just as true during choice time as it is during math or reading. For example, if children are counting by tens and seem confused, you step back and try a different approach to clarify the confusion. Similarly, if children seem lost when they're surrounded by the art materials you've supplied, you step back and do some more demonstration.

There are no absolute answers to most questions that will arise during choice time. However, if you strive for consistency and are open to innovation, creativity, and a culture of collaboration, you'll be ready to make in-the-moment decisions that honor the unique and special characteristics of your students. What follows are some helpful strategies and suggestions you might consider when you are faced with common challenges.

Center:
Instructional rationale for setting up this center:
Materials and physical setup of the center: (You might include a sketch of the layout of the center.)
What materials can be added to support inquiry and exploration in this center? (Add this information after observing how children are using the center.)
Are there any connections that can be made between this center and classroom studies and inquiry projects?

Figure 3.7. Planning Tool for Centers

My children don't have enough stamina to stay in a center.

When worried about students' stamina, consider exchanging the word *stamina* with the words *engagement and motivation*. In *Reading with Meaning* (2002), Debbie Miller explains how children's engagement is fueled by their motivation to read books on topics that interest them. Her students also trust her to provide them with engaging books they can read independently if they are motivated to work at making sense of the text (41). Similarly, if you pay close attention to your students and provide them with materials tied to their interests, motivation and engagement during choice time will thrive.

While sustained focus and engagement is developmental and a natural part of the learning process, even very young children will stay with an activity for a long period of time if they are motivated. To support her children's continued exploration of seeds and tree branches, Amy Binin set out some intriguing tools such as goggles, sandpaper-covered blocks, and vegetable peelers. The four-year-old students were engaged in their exploration for the entire hour. They were working intensely and intentionally as they attempted to scrape the "skin" off the bark to discover what was underneath. With very young children, you'll need to have patience and trust that they will develop focus over time.

Should children move from one center to another during choice time, or just stay in the one center they chose for the day?

Prekindergarten children, as Chip Wood describes in his book *Yardsticks*, are still at the stage of development where they will naturally move from one activity to another. They respond well to having the flexibility of making more than one choice each day. They are experimenting and interacting with the variety of cognitive and social possibilities presented by the different centers. As children get older, we place more emphasis on their concentration and engagement in each of the centers. By the time children are in kindergarten, first, and second grade, we can expect them to stay at their chosen center for the entire period rather than shifting from one activity to another. You can make this more easily possible by setting up centers that invite a variety of opportunities for creative play and explorations. It's not unusual for a child to declare that he is finished with a center, so here's where you can step in and point out some interesting materials that he may not have explored. You might even suggest that you come up with ideas together for adding new materials to the center. Your interventions show the child that you trust and respect his ability to extend his explorations and that you value his ideas and suggestions.

If you are going to assume that children will stay at one center rather than wandering from one to the other, it's important to have a plan for how this practice will be introduced. At the start of the year, you might schedule a relatively short choice time so that children ask for *more* time rather than wonder what to do at their centers after ten or fifteen minutes. Eventually, choice time will extend to forty-five minutes or an hour depending upon your schedule. By late winter and spring children are often so engaged in their play and explorations that they might continue in the same center for two, sometimes three, consecutive days. Of course there are always times when rules need to be bent or broken. There are times when a child is having, for one reason or another, a particularly difficult day and you might feel that it's best to make an accommodation. I've found, over my years of teaching, that children are particularly sensitive to the special needs of their classmates and your deviation from the choice time procedure will be well understood.

What can I do about children who don't behave?

First, remember that choice time should not be used to reward or punish children. Every child has a right to time for free play and exploration, just as each has a right to reading, writing, and math instruction. All sorts of important academic, social, and emotional learning happen as children engage together in centers, and no child should lose this opportunity.

You might consider having a cooling-off chair or a quiet area where a child who is struggling can spend a few minutes to reflect and get ready to reenter an activity. It's helpful if children see this as a positive, helpful option for them. After all, we all need a quiet spot in which to gather ourselves every now and then.

If a particular child seems to have lots of challenges, leave a few minutes each day to observe how he or she interacts at play during choice time. If you notice something that is frustrating the child, consider whether you can make modifications at the center that will remove the frustration and better support the child. You might also reintroduce the center in a way that will help the child be more successful.

How do I manage centers if I'm the only adult in the room?

Sometime in the 1980s, for fiscal reasons, many schools cut back on assistants and paraprofessionals in classrooms. Luckily, I often had parents who volunteered one hour a week to help with centers, and sometimes I had student teachers. Nevertheless, there were weeks when I was the only adult in the room, so I learned how to improvise to make my centers work under those conditions.

Make sure that all the materials children need are already in the centers and don't require an adult to set them out or up. Next, eliminate choices that require adult supervision for safety reasons (woodworking, for example) and then modify the more complicated centers. For example, in a cooking center, instead of making pancakes or carrot cake (which requires heat), children can squeeze oranges and then strain the juice. A simple recipe chart can lead them through the steps, and they can use plastic forks to cut the oranges. Look on the Internet for recipes that don't require cooking.

Don't open centers that need your undivided attention for the full period. For example, you might spend ten minutes making play dough with a group of children and then leave them to visit children in other centers. After you've moved on, the children who made the play dough can put away the ingredients and wash the mixing and measuring tools.

Finally, use your minilessons to teach children strategies for helping each other and staying safe during choice time. Invite children to help you create simple how-to charts for various centers. Include important safety rules such as "Always wear goggles to protect your eyes when working at the take-apart center."

How do I make the best use of parent volunteers during choice time?

I was lucky to have parents who volunteered to help in my classroom. I *thought* that everything was going well until I received a note from Sarah's mother, Emily.

Dear Renée,

I can now proudly admit that I have often felt helpless and have been clueless working with the kids at choice time. While I am aware of what needs to be accomplished, I am never quite sure how to get the kids to accomplish what needs to be done. No doubt, I have been very appreciative of the support you provide— stepping in, providing hints and tips—but honestly sometimes the minutes seem like hours. . . .

I was devastated! Emily had always appeared to be so happy when working with children in different centers. I then wondered if other parent helpers felt the same. Since there wasn't a time when I could meet with all the volunteers together, I settled for writing notes to help guide them. Here is some of the information I included in each note:

- the center they would be working in and the number of children that might be at that center
- a few sentences describing the center and how children might use the materials
- the role of a facilitator—not a doer, but an enabler—and some examples of open-ended questions
- a clear expectation that if there was a conflict that the children could not solve together, or if behavior got out of hand, I should be notified right away—any type of disciplining should be my responsibility.

4

> "My heart belonged to blocks. With those wooden blocks I was able to build bridges, skyscrapers, and even spaceships. I could feel the structural integrity of my creations, even if that meant sitting on them until they collapsed. Why was this satisfying? I don't know. All I knew was that crayons and books couldn't hold a candle to blocks!"
>
> —**Daniel,** remembering his year in kindergarten

Block Center

Raymond, Eleanor, and Carl *choose to work in the block center and decide to build castles. Their teacher suggests they search the Internet for interesting castle images. They find several castles they like, print the images, tape the printed images to the wall of the block center, and begin building.*

Raymond (Pointing to one of the photographs): *I like the bottom of this castle. I think we should change what we have to make it more like this. Maybe the castle won't fall down again if we change it.*

Eleanor: *Yeah. But how can we change it? I don't want to take this one down. We worked on it forever!*

Carl: *Let's destroy it!* (He stands up, ready to knock over the blocks.)

Raymond (Quickly intervening): *No! We don't have to change the whole thing. Let's just stop! Stop! What if we put the big blocks around it to protect it? Then maybe the small blocks won't fall so much.*

Carl: *OK. I'll get the big blocks.*

Eleanor: *Just be careful. Last time you knocked it down!* (Carl grimaces at Eleanor and starts to pile many big blocks in his arms at once.) *Give me some of those. I'll help you.*

Raymond: *We might not need that many.*

Eleanor: *Yes we do, if we want to put them around the whole castle. This castle is big!*

(As Carl places the big blocks next to the castle, the structure starts to shake.) *Oh no!*

Carl (Laughing): *Destruction!*

Raymond: *Wait! Move back! Don't let it fall!*

Eleanor: *I told you to be more careful!*

Carl (Still laughing): *This is awesome! It's gonna fall! It's gonna fall!*

Eleanor: *No! Make it stop!* (The blocks don't fall.)

Raymond: *See, the big blocks are working. They protected the small blocks.*

Eleanor: *That's not what happened. He just got lucky.*

Carl: *Let's put more blocks around.*

Raymond: *We can pretend that's the reason, though.*

The children continue to bolster their castle by surrounding it with blocks.

If you watch a group of children building towers, spaceships, and castles in the block center, you will see them developing in so many important ways—physically, mentally, and socially. First, children who are building with blocks are physically active. Raymond, Eleanor, and Carl are in almost constant motion—getting blocks, arranging blocks, and playing with the castle while it's being constructed and after it's built. The children are also mentally engaged as they propose and revise plans (*What if we put the big blocks around it to protect it?*) and as they reflect on what is and isn't working (*See, the big blocks are working. They protected the small blocks.*). And like all children who build together with blocks, Raymond, Eleanor, and Carl deal with interpersonal challenges and learn to collaborate and negotiate with others (*No! We don't have to change the whole thing. Let's just stop! Stop!*).

Children who are building with blocks are also developing many conceptual, disciplinary understandings related to their play. Raymond, Eleanor, and Carl experiment with balance, stability, and aesthetic appreciation as they arrange blocks on top of or next to one another. They practice mathematical and scientific thinking as they classify blocks according to size, weight, and shape or as they search for just the right piece to add to a structure (see Figure 4.1). They become familiar with geometric shapes such as triangles, arcs, rectangles, and squares. And they practice communication skills as they collaborate and negotiate while building a structure together.

The unit blocks used in most schools today were designed in the early nineteen hundreds by the progressive educator Caroline Pratt, who said of them, "I sought . . . something so flexible, so *adaptable*, that children could use it without guidance or control. I wanted to see them build a world; . . . to see them re-create on their own level the life about them" ([1948] 2014, 28). Pratt used Friedrich Froebel's geometric building blocks as her models. Froebel, a German educator in the eighteen hundreds, was the originator of the concept of kindergarten—"children's garden." Froebel's blocks had a great influence on the work of the architect Frank Lloyd Wright and on such visual artists as Piet Mondrian and Wassily Kandinsky (Brosterman 1997). Froebel's blocks, made to be used on a tabletop, fit together in different configurations, rather like a puzzle.

Figure 4.1. "What can I do with this block?"

Pratt created blocks that could be used on the floor and that were conducive to open-ended, creative play (Gadzikowski 2013). It turned out that moving block play to the floor made a big difference. As the industrial designer Tucker Viemeister (Colman 2008) explains, the unit blocks—with nothing to hold them together and difficult to move when assembled—encourage a more fluid, open-ended process that is never quite finished and easily started anew. For children like Raymond, Eleanor, and Carl to experience the full benefit of this more fluid, open-ended process in the block center, it's essential that the space, materials, and routines for the center be carefully planned.

Setting Up the Block Center

Space and Location

Deciding where to set up a block center in a busy classroom requires careful consideration, perhaps more than any other center you will plan. The center is a busy, active space filled with structures that are easily toppled, and young children are still developing their sense of spatial awareness. Some of them have a good sense of where they are in the physical space around them, while others are not yet secure in this understanding. As you plan for the center, you have to keep these differences in mind and support children as they learn to manage themselves in the space.

It probably goes without saying, but the more open space you can give children to build with blocks, the better. The amount of space affects the quality of the structures, as well as the quality of the children's collaboration. Ideally, the block area will be large enough that children can walk around their constructions and reach the block shelf without knocking the structures over (see Figure 4.2). If the space is too cramped, blocks will be accidentally knocked over, feelings will be hurt,

Figure 4.2. The center's size and design make this big building possible.

and there will be conflicts and tears. Not every setting is ideal, but there are compromises you can make. If the classroom is very small and there just isn't a large space to house the block center, children may need to work in pairs or threesomes rather than groups of four, five, or six. Another alternative is to have children work with blocks on the carpet in the meeting area. They'll have lots of space in this area to build, but it will prohibit them from working on structures over a number of days and therefore limit the block-building possibilities.

As far as location, the block area should be in a protected yet visible space: protected so that structures don't accidently get knocked down by someone walking from one part of the room to another and visible because children enjoy looking at their classmates' work. Often, the structures in the block area spark interesting observations and comments, and these conversations may lead children who were initially reluctant to play in the center to participate.

Whether or not the location is carpeted makes a difference as well. Not using a carpet in the block area makes it easier for children to balance the blocks; it's discouraging when blocks continually teeter. On the other hand, it's noisier when the blocks fall down (and they will!) on a hard floor, but it's a good noise, the noise of activity, sometimes accompanied by a groan, sometimes by hysterical laughter. And the children are unfazed; structures get rebuilt, often with design improvements! Out of preference or necessity, if you decide to have a rug in the block area, a flat rug with no nap is best. Also, avoid rugs with designs; they are distracting and can limit original building ideas.

Basic Materials

Begin the year with just enough different kinds of blocks (four or five shapes are a good number to begin) to make simple structures. When children are adept at using the blocks and know they need to return the blocks to the shelves or baskets when they take their structures apart, you can begin adding more material options. Placing labels on shelves ahead of time for soon-to-be-added materials will generate interest.

Here are some other basic materials you might consider for the block center:

- a ruler and a tape measure, which encourage children's fascination with measuring their constructions as they build (see Figure 4.3)
- photos of interesting structures on the walls in the center

- a basket of books containing illustrations and photographs of a variety of architectural structures
- a camera to photograph children's constructions (You can teach children to do this themselves as the year progresses.).

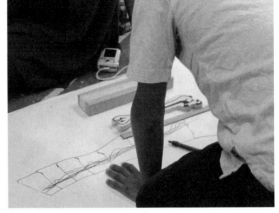

Figure 4.3. A first-grade child uses a ruler in the block center to make a skeleton.

Organization

The materials in the block center can be organized in a number of different ways, but there are some predictable management issues that can be solved with thoughtful planning and layout. First, consider placing the blocks on shelves on *opposite* sides of the center. This arrangement addresses the problem of children crowding the shelves and accidently knocking over blocks as they walk around another child's structure to get more blocks for their own. Also, consider defining the space with a line of tape on the floor. Position the line about a foot in front of the shelves and remind children not to build between the line and the shelves.

Labeling the shelves with images of the various block shapes lets children know where to find and return particular blocks. You can trace each block on black contact paper, cut out the shape, and affix the shape to the appropriate shelf or container (see Figure 4.4). Peter Napolitano, a kindergarten teacher in Manhattan, uses plastic bins to hold small shapes like the triangles and half circles. He puts shape labels on the bins as well as on the shelves where the bins belong. Any labeling you can do will make cleaning up much easier. An added bonus to arranging and labeling the blocks by size is that it helps children begin to make mathematical connections between them: *There are no more long*

Figure 4.4. The labeled block shelves let children know where to find and return blocks.

blocks. I'm going to try two of the shorter blocks next to the long ones. Maybe that will work.

Safety Guidelines

Because unit blocks are made of heavy wood, there must be rules for how they are used. Children also need to understand why you are serious about making sure they follow the rules. Elisabeth S. Hirsch, in her wonderfully informative resource *The Block Book* (1984), lists a number of rules children who use the block center must follow, including these three essentials:

- Never walk on the blocks. You might fall and hurt yourself or cause your structure to collapse.
- Never throw the blocks. Someone might get hurt, or something might get broken.
- Take your structures apart from top to bottom so they won't crash. Never kick a structure down.

It's probably best to start with just a few essential rules like these because you don't want them to overwhelm the children. As Hirsch says, "the rules are here to help us, not to enslave us!" (94). Consider your space, your particular group of children, and the specific materials you have in the center as you decide what the rules will be.

Figure 4.5. How high can you build?

You also need to decide how high you will allow children to build, as they will almost certainly test the limits when it comes to the height of their structures (see Figure 4.5). Some teachers tell children that constructions can be only as high as they can reach when they are standing on the floor. Others allow children to stand on a chair to place high blocks. When making this decision, consider students' age and maturity and know that whatever you decide, sometimes rules need to be broken. In my classes, I had a rule that structures could be built only as high as the children could reach. However, one group was building the World Trade Center and wanted to put a dowel on top to represent the aerial. I gave a child permission to stand on a chair (but stood nearby just in case).

Cleanup Guidelines

Before you ever launch the block center, it's important to think about the structures and routines you will use for cleaning up the space at the end of each session. You don't want picking up all the blocks to overwhelm children and discourage them from using the center, and it's easy to make block cleanup fun rather than tiresome. First, plan to conclude block play five minutes before the end of the session so cleanup isn't rushed. Then establish a routine. You might have each child randomly choose an index card on which a block shape is drawn and return all the blocks of that shape to the proper shelf. Alternatively, encourage children to form a line and pass the blocks to the person closest to the shelf. Or, let children problem solve the cleanup routine for themselves, as they are often quite adept at coming up with their own strategies. One of my groups decided to use a chair as a cart; they piled blocks on the seat and then pushed the chair to the appropriate shelf. If it works, it's good. If it works and it's fun, it's wonderful! Children are also tickled if you lend a hand.

Just as we encourage children to add on to writing pieces as the year proceeds, so will we nudge children toward drawing building plans and working on structures over the course of a few days. To support and encourage big thinking in the block center, structures are often left intact until the builders have completed their project.

Launching the Block Center

Once you've settled on all the logistics of setting up the block center and have them in place, it's time to plan how you will introduce the center to the class. As with most centers, it's best to launch it over a series of days so you build enthusiasm for the activities of the center. Whatever you plan, it's important to introduce children to the materials and also the play and exploration possibilities they will find in the center. While there are many ways a block center launch could go, here's a tried-and-true method you might consider, especially if this is your first time.

Begin by gathering the children in a circle in the block center (or the class meeting area if the block center is small). Have children, one by one or in pairs, choose a block, go to the center of the circle, and place it down any way they like. Explain that the block can stand up tall or lay down flat and can be straight or diagonal (a great new word!). After the first block is placed, the next child or pair adds another, and the only rule is that the two blocks have to touch. You might suggest different possibilities: the block could stand on top of the first one, lay on the floor right next to it, stand up tall next to it, and so on. Continue until each child or pair has had a turn.

As the structure grows, talk with the children about how it is changing: *It looks like a house! It doesn't look like a house anymore. It's a big tower!* This discussion can become quite animated! You might take photos or have children make some quick sketches of the changing construction. Since photos and drawings will look different depending on where children are sitting and what they see, this is a great opportunity to introduce the concepts of perspective and vantage point.

After two or three days of building with blocks together as a whole class, add the block center to the activities students can undertake on their own. Giving all the children the opportunity to handle the blocks helps everyone feel more confident about choosing this center and working there productively. As you introduce new materials in the center during the year, you might repeat this whole-class activity as a way of generating new possibilities.

Spotlight on Inquiry-Driven Centers

On the morning I visited Mary Anne Sacco's second-grade class, the children were studying New York City. The previous week they had taken two field trips. They had visited the New York Historical Society to learn about life during colonial days, and they had also visited Wave Hill, a large public garden and ecology center that overlooks the Hudson River.

Responding to these two experiences, the children suggested some centers they'd like to have for choice time. The day of my visit was the first day for these centers: blocks, watercolors, maps, and Legos. When center time began, the children appeared to be working parallel to each other with very little interaction or planning. In some areas, particularly blocks, there was some arguing and grabbing of blocks. Mary Anne and I chose not to intervene, but we were concerned about the lack of engagement and collaboration.

After about ten minutes, something amazing began to happen. Each group of children figured out a way to work together. The children in the block center began building sites in New York City, including an elevated highway one of the boys knew existed in the borough of Queens. At the map center, two of the girls started on a three-dimensional map of the city (see Figure 4.6). They didn't know about relief maps, but they worked out their own version by drawing, cutting out, and stuffing the borough of Manhattan.

At the Lego center, two children worked together to construct a colonial house. The children

Figure 4.6. Second graders planning a three-dimensional map of Manhattan

at watercolors decided to paint images of the Hudson River (without any knowledge of the Hudson River School of painting!).

In centers planned around their own interests, the children worked without adult intervention on their own inquiry projects and found their way toward collaboration and engagement.

Enhancing and Enriching the Block Center

Once children are using all the blocks on the shelves and understand the cleanup process, add more blocks (more of the shapes already there and also new shapes, such as triangles or arches). Mark the shelves with each new shape, and perhaps bring the new shapes to a class meeting, show them to the children, and ask the children to put the blocks on the shelves.

Over time, as you watch children build in the center, you will almost certainly have ideas for materials you could add that would enrich children's building possibilities. For example, you might add some of these items:

- small models of people and animals (Do this thoughtfully: the wrong prop can skew students' play in ways you haven't intended.)
- dollhouse furniture, small cars, or fire trucks (Some children may be intimidated by the blocks or initially disinterested. Adding something familiar might entice them to explore the center.)
- a basket containing adhesive tape, markers, pencils, index cards, sticky notes, and writing paper (Children can use these materials to put up signs, label structures with their names, and write messages about their structures. See Figure 4.7 for an example.)
- road maps and travel brochures to inspire children to build highways, cars, airplanes, and boats
- photos of structures created by students in previous years
- hard hats
- a basket of pieces of fabric.

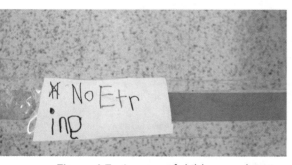

Figure 4.7. A group of children used writing materials to make a sign: No Entering!

In addition to adding materials, another way to enhance the work in the center is to encourage group projects. After children have had lots of time to investigate block-building possibilities, you might put up a large blank sheet of mural paper (or a whiteboard or chalkboard) on which children can draw collaborative building plans (see Figures 4.8 and 4.9).

Figure 4.8. Children list elements to include in their block plan.

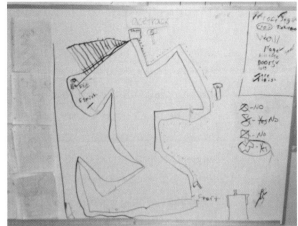

Figure 4.9. Children collaborate to draw their block plan on the whiteboard.

As children build structures in the block center, individually or collaboratively, observe how they use the materials and interact with one another. Take notes and photographs and draw quick sketches; then use them to create a documentation panel to display in the block center. This visual representation enriches and extends the work of the center in so many ways. It helps you and the children reflect on the work they are doing and inspires continued collaboration and innovation. Encourage children who are invested in a building project to invite classmates to work with them. They can continue working on their project as many days as is needed for it to be completed.

The block center can also enrich social studies projects throughout the year. If you are studying bridges, add yarn or string for making suspension bridges or pulleys for making moveable bridges. Classes exploring supermarkets can create one based on photographs and sketches from field trips and illustrations in books (see Figure 4.10).

Figure 4.10. A block supermarket

Teaching Interventions in the Block Center

As children are engaged in the play and exploration of the center, teaching interventions based on your observations will support children's explorations and can make all the difference in the richness of their experience. For example, when the block center is new, it's not unusual for children to play side by side rather than interact in pairs or groups. This type of *parallel play* won't last long, especially if you encourage children to build together. A comment such as "Sammy, I wonder if your long train track can go to Suzie's house" may be just what Sammy and Suzie need to begin constructing together. The key is to learn to observe with an eye toward an intervention that makes sense based on the context and also where you hope to take children in their work together. The Teaching Interventions chart will give you some ideas about typical scenarios in a block center and possible interventions.

Block Play as a Way into Children's Emotional Lives

As with any dramatic play, sometimes the block area becomes a place for children to attend to their emotional lives and safely address what troubles them. Imagine this scene: Leonard has enclosed Karl inside what looks like a house without doors. Each time Karl's arm reaches out, a wooden block falls down on him and Leonard quickly replaces it. Then Leonard runs to the book nook, where we have a collection of stuffed animals, selects one, returns to the block building, and passes a stuffed animal to Karl. They repeat this over and over, and Karl's collection of animals grows. Curious about what this is all about, I walk over to the blocks and ask Leonard about his building. "Karl is in jail, but don't be worried. I bring him toys so he won't be scared." Block building is giving Leonard a safe outlet for expressing his fears for his father, who is in jail.

Teaching Interventions

Observation	Possible Response
Children worked hard on a construction and planned to continue with it the next day. When they return to school, they discover that other children who use the classroom for an after-school program have knocked over the structures, and the block builders are angry and upset.	First recognize and empathize with their situation. Then ask if they can think of a solution. You might ask whether they think a sign and some kind of barrier might be helpful.
Children are bumping into one another and accidentally knocking over structures. Tempers are high. Tears are flowing.	Call a class meeting to discuss the problem and brainstorm solutions. You could have just three children use the center instead of four, or make the block center bigger and an adjoining center smaller. Often children will come up with solutions you haven't thought of, so begin a conversation that focuses on the importance of their voices in resolving the conflict.
Children are building and rebuilding the same structures every time they work in the block center.	In a minilesson, introduce books that have illustrations of interesting structures. Add graph paper to the center on which children can plan new buildings and document them when they are completed. Remind builders to add any new details to their building plans. This presents an opportunity to use the term *revision* and refer to the revisions they make on their writing pieces during writing workshop.

continues

Observation	Possible Response
The same children keep going to the block center. You want to interest others, particularly children who have been avoiding this activity.	Add new materials to the center, such as dollhouse furniture and small animals, cars, and trains. Think about what will appeal to the children who have been avoiding the center.
Block center cleanup is chaotic. You realize that children have been avoiding the block center because they don't want to have to clean up the blocks.	Encourage children to put away blocks that are not part of their constructions so that the area doesn't become overrun with blocks. Attach rope handles to milk crates that children can then use as block-moving vehicles. Each child can fill up a vehicle, drive it to the shelves, and put the blocks away.

Another Option: Setting Up a Block Room

If your school has an unused classroom or storeroom, it can become a block room shared by several teachers. This works particularly well with first and second graders who are working on big collaborative projects. In one combined block/inquiry room in a New York City school, teams of children painted murals, constructed models, and created structures that extended their social studies projects. A group of first graders in the school studying the New York City subway system used the blocks to build subway tracks and stations. They also painted murals for the stations and constructed subway cars.

For example, here's how one block room is set up and implemented:

- The floor is taped off into distinct square areas large enough for groups of three or four children to work together cooperatively.
- Individual teachers sign up for their class to use the room for a week at a time.
- Children in the class work together on a class project generally connected to something the class has been studying.

- Children in each class split into building groups or committees and together sketch their portion of the project and create lists of the materials they will need.
- Teachers document the progression of the work so children can reflect on the experience.
- Documentation is shared and discussed during class meetings so children have a sense of what has been done and what needs to be done.
- When the project is completed, the children and teachers share it (including their plans and drawings) with the school community.

5

Science is a way of thinking much more than it is a body of knowledge.

—Carl Sagan

Science Center

On the day *a water table has been added to Mary Ellen Musacchia's kindergarten science center, Michael, David, Blessed, and Joshua are experimenting. Michael, using an ice cream scoop to fill a watering can, repeats to himself, "Scoop it up! Scoop it up!"*

David joins Michael and they exchange the scoop for small cups as they continue filling the can together. David, jumping with excitement, urges Michael to "get it to the top." Michael peeks into the can and decides, "It needs more." When the can is full, they pick it up together, pour the water over a waterwheel and jump gleefully as the wheel begins to spin.

Blessed is struggling to operate a small pump. David moves over to help her. "It's easy to do. Look, Blessed. That's how you do it. See?"

Joshua is squirting water onto the waterwheel from a small squeeze bottle. "I have water. Who needs some water?"

"Me," Blessed responds. "Squirt harder so the wheel goes faster!"

Filling and pouring, again and again, the four children are fascinated with the power of the water and the power of themselves, the pourers.

Young children are natural scientists who experiment, investigate, observe, and question the world around them. They look closely at a snail as it slowly crawls across a table. They drop leaves into a water table and wonder why they don't sink to the bottom. They feel a sense of excitement and power when they discover they can make a wheel spin by pouring water on it. For young children, the whole world is a laboratory. In a science center, we bring the outside world into the classroom and then give children the tools and materials they need to explore it as scientists.

Figure 5.1. Closely observing a worm

Playing independently with a waterwheel in the science center, Michael, David, Blessed, and Joshua naturally engage in many of the eight scientific practices required by the NEXT GENERATION SCIENCE STANDARDS* (NGSS):

1. Asking questions and defining problems
2. Developing and using models
3. Planning and carrying out investigations
4. Analyzing and interpreting data
5. Using mathematics and computational thinking
6. Constructing explanations and designing solutions
7. Engaging in argument from evidence
8. Obtaining, evaluating, and communicating information.

The children engage in these practices in developmentally appropriate ways. With support from their teacher, in a variety of different explorations across

---

* Next Generation Science Standards is a registered trademark of Achieve. Neither Achieve nor the lead states and partners that developed the Next Generation Science Standards was involved in the production of, and does not endorse, this product.

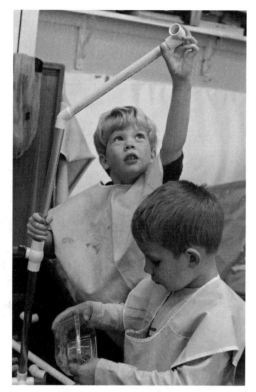

Figure 5.2. Experimenting with water

the year, they can learn to use all these practices to experience the world as scientists.

Significantly, Michael, David, Blessed, and Joshua are also demonstrating many of the habits of mind that are characteristic of intelligent human behavior (see text box on this page). By sticking to the task of filling up the watering can and causing the wheel to spin, they exhibit persistence. Using a squirt bottle, a water pump, and cups, they think flexibly and generate alternative methods for solving a problem. David listens with empathy and understanding and, seeing Blessed's frustration in working the pump, teaches her how to use it. Continuing to play and explore, these children work together interdependently. From their excitement, it's obvious they are responding with wonderment and awe as they figure out strategies for using water to move the wheel.

In their book *Habits of Mind Across the Curriculum: Practical and Creative Strategies for Teachers* (2009) Arthur Costa and Bena Kallick identify sixteen habits of mind that intelligent humans use when confronted with problems to which the resolutions are not immediately apparent:

1. Persisting
2. Managing impulsivity
3. Listening with understanding and empathy
4. Thinking flexibly
5. Thinking about thinking (metacognition)

6. Striving for accuracy

7. Questioning and posing problems

8. Applying past knowledge to new situations

9. Thinking and communicating with clarity and precision

10. Gathering data through all senses

11. Creating, imagining, innovating

12. Responding with wonderment and awe

13. Taking responsible risks

14. Finding humor

15. Thinking interdependently

16. Remaining open to continuous learning

It's easy to imagine how children working together in a science center would be supported in all the habits of mind identified by Costa and Kallick (2009) and the eight essential practices of the NGSS across the year. A science center is a place of rich discovery where children take on the personas of scientists and experiment with a variety of materials. In this chapter you'll learn how to establish a dynamic, exciting science center where children will flourish as they grow and develop as scientists and intelligent problem solvers.

Establishing a Science Center for Young Children

When a teacher working in a school near the seashore opened his science center at the start of the school year, he considered the children who would soon join him in his classroom. His school is only a short walk to the bay in one direction and the ocean in the other, so he knew his students would have firsthand knowledge and experience of the seashore. During the summer, he collected seashells, which he set out in the science center in September to spark the first investigation.

Before opening the center, the teacher shared the shells with the children during a class meeting. First he asked whether the shells made them think about their summer vacation and invited children to share their stories and memories. Then, in pairs, they examined a few of the shells, followed by a class discussion: "Do we have any ideas why the shells don't all look alike? What similarities did you notice? Who noticed something about a shell that was surprising?" The teacher recorded all their observations and responses.

As the class revisited their observations at the next day's meeting, one of the children commented that some of the shells were smooth and some were bumpy. The teacher responded, "I wonder why all of the shells are not smooth?" He then invited children to share things they wondered about and recorded them on the chart they'd started the day before.

Finally, on the third day, the new science center opened and the children who chose to study the shells were invited to search for answers to some of the wonderings their classmates had expressed. The chart was posted in the center, and whenever children made discoveries that answered any of the questions, they shared this information at a class meeting. Because these first graders were beginning to do a lot of independent writing, their teacher created a bulletin board space headed "Scientific Discoveries," where children could post written answers to particular questions.

Plan with Students in Mind

When planning the focus for your first science center, it's helpful to think about your students and the experiences they will mostly likely bring with them to school. This is important because if children can access prior knowledge, it will help them feel successful in their first explorations in the center. Since your geographic location is the one thing all your students will have in common, it's a good place to start planning. Seashells made sense for this group of students who live so close to the ocean, but shells are probably not the best choice for children in the middle of rural Iowa. A soil or rock exploration would likely be a better fit in such a location.

Make sure the materials you choose for the center are easy to obtain and inexpensive, and that they are open-ended enough for children to be innovative in their explorations (see Figures 5.3 and 5.4).

It's also important that children be able to work with the materials both independently and safely. If you have to hover too close as children first use the center, they will come to depend on you to be there to guide their investigations. While every group of children is different, here are some tried-and-true materials and topics that reflect the interests and curiosity of most children:

- seashells, snails, and hermit crabs
- magnets
- seeds and pods
- leaves, branches, tree pods
- plants and flowers
- water
- color
- sand, pebbles, and rocks
- life cycles (butterflies; frogs; mealworms)
- baby chicks in an incubator
- bird feathers, bones, and nests
- shadows
- insects

Figure 5.3. Twigs and stones arranged for exploration

Without a doubt, after just a few weeks in school, you will have all kinds of ideas for science explorations that make sense for your particular group of children and their interests. The possibilities are really endless, and very often new ideas arise from children's questions. For example, in April 2010, one of my first-grade students brought in a newspaper article about the Deepwater Horizon oil spill. As we discussed the article, the children were both disturbed and fascinated by the challenge of cleaning up the water. We decided to become oil-cleanup scientists and conduct

Figure 5.4. A child explores twigs.

experiments in the science center. We filled pans with water and dripped varying amounts of oil into them, then tried to clean the oil from the water using a range of materials. The most successful straining implement turned out to be a bird's feather, which led us to wonder what happened to the ducks in the water. Did the oil stick to their feathers as it stuck to the feather in our experiment? This question led to more questions and research on the effects of oil spills on the natural environment. In the end, a group of children conveyed what they'd learned in a letter to the oil company responsible for the spill!

Supply the Center with Tools and Equipment

Once you've decided what students will be exploring in the science center, the next step is to decide which tools and equipment will best support their explorations. In the seashell study, for example, the center was equipped with a variety of basic tools and research supports. Children used magnifying glasses, rulers, tape measures, and balance scales to examine and compare the properties of different shells. They used egg cartons to sort the shells in different ways, and in blank books labeled "Seashell Explorations" they recorded their observations in words and drawings using graphite pencils, colored pencils, and crayons. And for secondary research there were photographs of seashells and mollusks as well as a basket of books about shells (including a shell handbook).

Books About Shells

- *Can You Find These Seashells?* by Carmen Bredeson
- *Who Lives in a Shell?* by Kathleen Weidner
- *Shells, Shells, Shells,* by Nancy Elizabeth Wallace
- *My Shell Book*, by Ellin Kirk
- *Seashells by the Seashore*, by Marianne Berkes
- *Sherman Swaps Shells*, by Jane Clarke

Basically, the tools you place in the center will depend on the properties of the materials children are exploring. Water explorations, for instance, will require different tools than seed explorations. Just as with materials, there are many, many tool possibilities, but here are some standard options:

- sorting trays, cups, or boxes
- microscopes (digital microscopes that can be projected on a screen are particularly effective)
- cameras
- timers and stopwatches
- funnels
- measuring cups and spoons
- plastic beakers or cups for pouring
- tweezers
- plastic bags
- eye droppers
- goggles
- lab coats (cut-down adult-size white shirts with stick-on labels for name tags work well)
- kitchen scale
- thermometers
- date stamps (for recording observations)
- nonfiction books and magazines.

In addition to having the tools and equipment needed to do scientific experiments, it's important that children collect data and observations just as all scientists do (see Figure 5.5). They can do this either in science notebooks they bring with them to the science center or in blank books kept in the center. In *Starting with Science: Strategies for Introducing Young Children to Inquiry*, Marcia Talhelm Edson explains, "When we talk about science notebooks in a preK, kindergarten, or primary classroom, we are building on the same structure used in professional scientists'

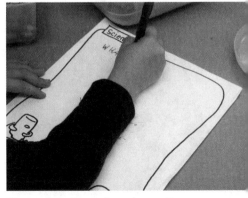

Figure 5.5. Recording observations in the science center

notebooks. These are working documents that enable children to record data and ideas and then use that data as evidence to develop theories, make judgments, raise questions, or share information with peers" (2013, 34).

To support children as they record observations and data, consider creating an illustrated word wall of significant words they'll need. One teacher I know put up a felt board and attached a piece of Velcro to the back of each word. Children could remove the words to use as a reference when writing. As studies change across the year, you can introduce new words that specifically support the different explorations.

Introduce the Center

To address the development of children's understanding, Jean Piaget wrote, "Children have real understanding only of that which they invent themselves, and each time that we try to teach them too quickly, we keep them from reinventing it themselves" (Pulaski 1970, 197). Whenever we've set up a new exploration in the science center, it's tempting to "teach too quickly" and send children off to explore without properly setting the stage. When you introduce a center to children over a series of days, you create anticipation and prompt more class discussion connected to the center. Children have time to mull over many ideas and possibilities before they actually get their hands on the materials and begin investigating.

There are lots of ways you might introduce a new center to the whole class. During a class meeting, you might share a book on the topic during read-aloud and talk about what children know about the topic and what they wonder. You might share some of the materials and tools from the center and have children share personal connections, as the teacher did with his seashell collection. A little excursion is a great way to build interest. If you're going to explore leaves, for example, you might first go on a neighborhood walk and have the children collect leaves in little bags, then share their findings with each other at a class meeting (see Figure 5.6). Basically any engagement that gets children

Figure 5.6. Collecting leaves and twigs for the science center

talking, thinking, and wondering about the new materials in the center will help build anticipation and interest. Be sure to chart children's questions so you have a record of them.

You might also take a day or two to introduce some of the tools in the center and demonstrate how they are used, especially if they're new or delicate (like a microscope). If it's the beginning of the year, consider showing children photographs of science laboratories or reading a book about them. Then, after discussing how important an orderly laboratory is for scientists, ask the children to help you devise practical instructions on how to care for the center and its materials and equipment. Participating in setting up the rules gives children a greater sense of agency.

During this introductory period, it's very important to model the kind of questioning that shows students how scientific discovery is built on a foundation of inquiry, investigation, and discourse. For example, if you were introducing birds' nests in the science center, you might pose questions like these: How big is it? What kinds of birds would fit in a nest like this? What is the nest made of? Which birds would have access to those materials? How might we find some answers to these questions? and Can we use any of the tools at the science center to learn more about the nest? This kind of thoughtful, pointed questioning models a scientific stance and enriches the study of science.

Ideally, by the time you officially open the center for children to visit, you will have some sort of chart filled with their questions and wonderings about the topic that is on display in the center, and the children will have a good sense of the kind of exploring and investigating that will happen there. Invite children to search for answers to their own and their classmates' questions.

Add New Materials as Needed

When a new center first opens, it's a good idea not to put out all the materials at once. Choose those you think will be most appealing and that will help children begin answering some of their questions. Then, as each exploration evolves, you can thoughtfully add new materials. Sometimes you'll see a need to add something right away, but usually you'll add materials as children's explorations become more sophisticated or as their interest in the existing materials wanes.

object	It looked like...	Under the microscope	notes
			Name Lionel
			Date 3/24/00
Fomic Bar			Flaked bumpy.
Brush			It looked like straw.
Nickle			I could almost feel the bumps.
erasor			Because of the pencil marks, there are little eyes.
feather			It looks like a laser beam.

Figure 5.7. Lionel's recording sheet

Imagine the seashell exploration, for example. The teacher might launch the center with a big collection of all types of small shells for children to study and then, after a few days, add in a very large conch shell to prompt new observations and questions. If the children seem particularly interested in measuring the shells, he could add strips of gridded oak tag paper on which they could arrange shells by size. If they seem fascinated by texture, he could add play dough or clay so the children could make impressions of shells. He might take the children on a field trip to the beach to collect even more shells, or he could add hermit crabs or snails to the center so the children could see shells protecting living animals.

You will see so many possibilities for extensions once children begin exploring in the center. As a matter of fact, if you have children share from their explorations often in whole-class meetings, they will surely come up with their own ideas for ways to extend these explorations. Thoughtfully adding new materials and tools to the center is one of the best ways to hold children's interests over time. Here are some general questions to guide you as you observe and think about those possibilities.

- Are children focusing on a particular task or element that could be supported by new materials or tools?
- Are they ready to manage more sophisticated recording techniques (pictographs, graphic organizers, scientific method templates, recording forms)? (See Figure 5.7.)
- Is there a way the exploration might move out of the classroom (field trip) so children could find new materials of their own to add?

Pay Close Attention to Questions

The role of questions throughout an inquiry is critical. You begin modeling a questioning stance when you introduce the center, and you continue modeling it as you interact with children in the center over time. In fact, in *Primary Science: Taking the Plunge*, Wynne Harlen suggests that a teacher's verbal questioning is "the most important factor in establishing a climate conducive to question asking by children" (2001, 39). The goal is to ask provocative, open-ended questions that stretch children's thinking and inspire thoughtful, personal responses. Consider the difference, for example, in the questions in the Teaching Interventions chart.

The differences in these questions are subtle but significant. Those on the left presume answers and those on the right presume possibilities and extend curiosity. In "On Listening to What Children Say," Vivian Gussin Paley (2007) suggests teachers model curiosity, not answers, and nowhere is that more important than when it's connected to children's scientific explorations.

Teaching Interventions

Questions That Presume Answers	Questions That Promote Exploration
How many speckled shells and how many striped ones do we have?	What do you discover if you arrange the shells by their different patterns?
Can you list the steps that show how a chrysalis turns into a butterfly?	How do you think you will know when the butterfly is ready to come out of the chrysalis?
How do you separate pebbles from soil?	What materials might you use to separate the pebbles from the soil?
Do you know why the face you've drawn on your shadow puppet isn't showing up on the screen?	What might you do to make a shadow that shows the eyes, nose, and mouth? Try some experiments with scraps of paper and see what happens.

Children will have questions of their own, of course, and their endless curiosity will fuel the center and determine the direction it will take. In a 2010 interview with Stephen Colbert, the astrophysicist Neil deGrasse Tyson described science as "a way of equipping yourself with the tools to interpret what happens in front of you," and said he believes strongly in supporting children's "scientific literacy," which is "the ability to show one's thinking" (see https://www.youtube.com/watch?v=bzf-yTj9RZc). Our response to children's questions and curiosity supports their developing scientific literacy and carries their playful explorations forward.

Having a place to record students' questions and wonderings is critical, and since you won't always be there when a question arises, it's helpful if children can add them on their own. Placing a pad of sticky notes next to a chart is a great way to accomplish this, and it allows you to move questions around on the chart, take them down, and add new ones. As a whole class, revisit the question chart often and talk about children's evolving understandings and, sometimes, their *mis*understandings. As you talk about the questions, ask children to explain their thinking. Over time, explaining their thinking will become second nature.

Often, young children state their questions as observations, and it takes some skill to recognize this and help them reframe their thinking. For example, I once observed a child at a water table take a thin paper cup and fill it with water. The cup quickly began to disintegrate, and in a frantic voice, the child said, "It's breaking! What's happening? My cup is in little pieces!" Instead of explaining that paper falls apart in water, this would be a wonderful opportunity to suggest the child explore how different materials react to being immersed in water. I might say, "You noticed that the paper cup fell apart in water. What would happen if you put one of our plastic snack cups or a coffee cup in the water? There are also metal cups in a pan under the water table. Can you experiment with different cups and decide which ones would be best for us to use at the water table?" A simple explanation would have shut down all inquiry, but reframing the child's observation in this way can spark new investigations.

Observe to Learn

Learning deepens over time. What you observe in the science center in September is probably not what you will be looking for in March. At the start of the year, you're trying to get a sense of what children already know and can do, information that will help you ascertain growth as you observe the children throughout the year. When school first begins, for example, you may not expect children to have the perseverance to retry an experiment in a new way if it doesn't work the first time; later in the year, this is something you'll be looking for.

As you observe children at the science center, you'll be thinking about group dynamics, or *how* children are working and playing together, and also about scientific literacy, or *what* children are learning and doing as scientists. Here are some general things to look for when you observe children at the science center:

Group Dynamics

- How are children interacting? Does the exploration encourage or discourage collaboration?
- Can I add or take away material to facilitate better collaboration and exploration?
- Are children losing interest in this exploration? Could a new exploration develop from this one?

Scientific Literacy

- Are children planning science experiments based on their personal questions or on the list of class wonderings?
- Are they conducting investigations to answer *Why? How?* and *What if I tried this?*
- Are they noticing and discussing changes? Similarities and differences?
- Are they using new science vocabulary in their conversations?
- Do they retry an experiment when it doesn't work the first time? Do they stick with an activity even though it is initially frustrating?
- Are they describing their findings? Are they finding ways to record their findings?
- Do they incorporate writing into their work?
- Do they refer to relevant nonfiction? Are there ways to incorporate more opportunities for reading?
- Are they using mathematical strategies (graphing their findings; using a scale to make comparisons; sorting objects according to size, shape, weight, or color)? (See Figure 5.8.)

Figure 5.8. Using a scale to weigh the class turtle

Spotlight on Inquiry-Driven Centers

When Barbara Matthews and Frances Sachdev were exploring the Full
Option Science System (FOSS) fabric module, they extended their whole-
class lessons by having children explore a variety of fabric textures and
weights in the science center. At the same time, the students visited a local
indoor marketplace as part of a social studies unit and were surprised to
see a clothing stall. Frances wondered out loud whether they could make
their own clothing for a class market the children were creating in the
dramatic play center. They began to brainstorm.

"We need fabrics of different colors," a child suggested, so they went
to the supermarket to buy the vegetables needed to make dyes. For
several days, children in the science center cooked beets and onions to
make dyes and learned how to color muslin fabric.

Next they wove their own fabrics using shoebox looms, yarn, and strips
of fabric remnants. They experimented to see which materials would
work together. They took risks, trying all sorts of nontraditional materials,
including pieces of rubber bands (they didn't work) and shoelaces.

The children made mistakes, and entire patches of weaving had to be pulled apart. But by creatively combining yarn and strips of material, they eventually formed an unusual fabric square, which they gave to the children in the art center, who glued it to dresses and shirts they had made from butcher paper. These were then displayed in the market in the dramatic play center.

Enhancing and Enriching the Science Center

The focus of the science center will shift and change across the year. You'll know it's time for a change if children have lost interest and are no longer choosing the center, of course. But more often than not, fulfilling the requirements of your science curriculum will lead to changes during the year. Extending your whole-class lessons with explorations in the science center is a great way to deepen children's understandings of the curriculum. You almost certainly won't have a problem figuring out what should come next when it's time for a change in the science center, but just in case, here are some suggestions for centers you might try if you're in search of new territory.

Take Something Apart

Taking an old, broken, or discarded machine apart and using the parts to create a new machine or sculpture encourages students to tinker with machinery and think creatively. Children love to dismantle literally anything mechanical—from vacuums to radios to computers. They'll need tools of course—screwdrivers and pliers, specifically—which means they'll also need goggles (very important). Be sure to demonstrate how to use the tools if they are new to the children. A box for sorting parts is also essential, as well as blank recording books for inventory and ideas. For secondary research, consider including a basket of appropriate books (for example, *Tools*, by Ann Morris; *The Toolbox*, by Ann Rockwell; *Toolbox*, by Gail Gibbons; and *Simple Machines*, by Cindy Davis).

As the children unscrew and examine the various parts, encourage them to think about the purpose of each part and the reasons for the overall design. You might introduce them to design drawings and invite them to draw the machine they're dismantling and also the new one they're planning to build. The key is to nudge them to explain their thinking and reasoning as they dismantle and reassemble. (See Figures 5.9 through 5.11.)

Figure 5.9. Working at the take-apart center

Construct Boats

After children have learned about the properties of water and the phenomena of sinking and floating, challenge them to construct boats that float using a variety of materials from the art center—clay, aluminum foil, Styrofoam, wood, and cardboard. After they have constructed a floating boat, encourage them to write a how-to-make-a-boat book to add to the science center.

Figure 5.10. Materials at the take-apart center

Find Out All About Snails

Snails are low-maintenance classroom pets that fascinate children. First read aloud a nonfiction book about snails and have the children prepare a habitat for garden snails. Once the snails arrive in the classroom, there are endless avenues of exploration. What do the snails like to eat? How do they eat? What are the parts of their bodies? How does the snail make slime? How do snails move? What will happen if we put a snail in a maze? Why are snails vegetarians?

Discover What Mixes with Water

Invite children to explore what can and cannot mix with water. They might record their experiments, noting materials used, predictions, procedures, and findings. Materials they could use include food coloring, vegetable oil, pepper, spices, food extracts, gelatin, powdered drink mixes, loose teas, and tea in bags. (See Figure 5.12.) They'll come up with additional suggestions!

Observe Animals

If the area near a class pet is set up for thoughtful observations, children will be eager to go to that center. Some simple classroom pets might be hermit crabs, fish, snails, insects, a bearded dragon, or a corn snake. (Hamsters and guinea pigs are soft and cuddly, but there might be children who are allergic to furry animals.) At an animal observation center, you might include any of the following:

- a basket of fiction and nonfiction books about the animal
- magnifying glasses and "detail finders" (a square of paper with a peephole in the center—wonderful for focusing on details)
- clipboards with paper or small notebooks for recording observations
- pencils for observational drawings
- colored pencils for adding specific details.

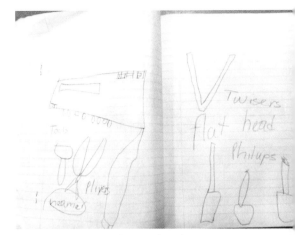

Figure 5.11. Recording at the take-apart center

Figure 5.12. Children explore what mixes with water at the wicking center.

Figure 5.13. A child's record of the behavior of Peter the turtle: "He follows your pencil."

Encourage children to engage in specific research when they are observing animals. When one of my first graders, Arkeimah, wanted to know if our class turtle, Peter, slept with his eyes closed, she observed him and also read through some of the nonfiction books on turtles located near his tank. Other children interested in how turtles eat took Peter out of his tank and placed him in a big tub on the rug. They enticed Peter to follow a carrot before giving it to him to eat as they observed him closely. (See Figure 5.13.)

> The issue is not to teach [a child] the sciences, but to give him [or her] the taste for loving them.
>
> —Jean-Jacques Rousseau

Reading Nook

Carl, Richard, and Sara *each pick a few books from the classroom library and go to the classroom "cozy corner," where they curl up on the beanbag chairs to read. Carl and Richard share a beanbag and read a dinosaur book together. Carl points to a picture and laughs: "Look in the bus; there are teddy bears." Richard begins chanting the familiar teddy bear song and Carl and Sara join in.*

Richard then says, "Turn the page!"

Carl does and exclaims, "Look!" He points at a picture of a dinosaur. "His eyes turn around and around when you move this thing."

He moves a tab in the book, and Richard says, "Turn it faster! He looks scary, like his eyes are rolling."

"Like a wild thing rolling his terrible eyes," Sara pipes in. "I don't like that book. It scares me."

Richard says, "OK, let's look at another book." Sara grabs a book about apples, Richard takes a Clifford book, and Carl chooses another dinosaur book. After reading silently for a while, they exchange books with one another. Sara returns to the page in the original dinosaur book that scared her. She moves the tab to roll the dinosaur's eyes, then quickly closes the book and pushes it away. She picks up the Clifford book and looks through the pages, retelling the story to herself.

As a child, I often sought out secret spots in our small city apartment—under a table, behind a chair, even the privacy of the bathroom—where I could read to my dolls without distraction. I sometimes imagined that Maude Hart Lovelace transported me to Deep Valley, Minnesota, to the world of Betsy and Tacy, the main characters in my favorite book series. As an adult, I love rainy weekends. In warm, sunny weather, I feel compelled to get outside and do something—walk, shop, visit a museum. But on rainy days I don't feel guilty about staying indoors, finding a cozy spot to settle, usually on my living-room couch, and losing myself in a good book. Like Anna Quindlen, for me, "reading continues to provide an escape from a crowded house into an imaginary room of [my] own" (1998, 31).

When I became a teacher, I wanted my students to have a comfortable, cozy hideaway where they could either read privately or share a book with a friend and have serious or giggly conversations. I wanted a place where children could go to mind-travel to the Hundred Acre Wood, climb to the land above the earth where Jack visits the Giant, or visit Peter and Willie on their street in Brooklyn. Creating a reading nook in a crowded, busy classroom sends an important message: it validates the value of losing oneself in literature.

In *The Reading Environment*, Aiden Chambers writes that "every reader knows that *where* we read affects *how* we read: with what pleasure and willingness and concentration. Reading in bed, feeling warm and comfortable and relaxed, is different from reading in a cold railway station waiting for a train, or in the sun on a crowded beach, or in a library full of readers, or alone in a favorite chair at ten o'clock in the morning" (1996, 1). He suggests, "If we want to be skillful in helping other people, especially children, become willing, avid, and—most important of all—thoughtful readers, we need to know how to create a reading environment that enables them" (1).

In the reading nook, Richard, Carl, and Sarah are experiencing a reading environment that is a miniworld of literacy. Together they read words, talk about pictures, compare books, write notes, and mark pages; they even sing in response to their reading! They also exhibit many important reading habits of mind (Billmeyer, in Costa 2009). Consider, for example, how the children are incorporating the following practices:

- *Applying past knowledge to new situations:* The children compare the dinosaur with pictures of monsters from another book the teacher previously read to them: "He looks scary, like his eyes are rolling" and "Like a wild thing rolling his terrible eyes."
- *Thinking and communicating with clarity and precision:* Sara's response to the rolling eyes of the dinosaur is clear. She doesn't want to share this book with her friends because it scares her.
- *Thinking interdependently:* The children have a shared knowledge of the teddy bear chant, which is started by Richard and picked up by the others. When they look at the next page of the dinosaur book, Carl notices the tab for moving the dinosaur's eyes and observes that it looks as if the eyes are rolling. Sara makes a connection to a book they have all previously heard read aloud, *Where the Wild Things Are.* They are creating their interpretation of a dinosaur as a wild thing.
- *Remaining open to continuous learning:* Sara returns to the book that frightened her to see whether she can manage reading it on her own. She can't, but she is open to the possibility.

Figure 6.1. Sharing books in the reading nook

A reading nook gives children a place to engage fully and independently as readers, joyfully and on their own terms (see Figure 6.1). It's an oasis in a noisy, active classroom, a place where children and books come together in so many powerful ways.

Setting Up a Reading Nook

A reading nook doesn't require a lot of space—you don't *want* a lot of room. The Merriam-Webster digital dictionary definition of a nook is "a small space or corner that is inside something." Your classroom reading nook should be small and cozy.

Teachers find many inventive ways to carve out a niche where children can cuddle up to read or have a special chat with a friend. Melissa Merriam couldn't seem to find space for a reading nook in her small room, but necessity is the mother of invention. By emptying out the lower part of a closet, moving in some child-size easy chairs, and replacing the door with a sheer, filmy curtain, she created a lovely spot. The finishing touches were children's family photos taped to the walls. (See Figures 6.2 and 6.3.) Her students truly owned this space.

A teacher at PS 10 in Brooklyn had her students help set up a reading corner. At a morning meeting she introduced the idea of creating a special place for quiet reading. The children shared stories about where they liked to read when they were not at school. Some children made drawings of themselves reading in their special reading spots. Others looked through magazines for pictures of children reading. Then they got to work. They arranged a few small chairs, a little sofa, and some pillows around a bookrack, put favorite storybooks in the bookrack, and filled a few baskets with more books. They created a reading frieze to post on the wall and put up a sign saying Come and Read. Their book nook was open and ready for reading and sharing books (see Figure 6.4).

I often turned a big refrigerator carton into a private reading or conversation space. A neighbor who was a carpenter built a sturdy frame for the inside. An arch cut

Figure 6.2. Even a closet can become a book nook.

Figure 6.3. A comfortable chair makes a big difference.

into the front panel created an entrance, and a "skylight" let in light. The floor was cushioned with a pillow and a blanket. Children were eager to spend a free-choice period reading there. The first year I asked the children to help name it. *Quiet* and *cozy* were the words they used most frequently to describe it, so it became our Quiet, Cozy Reading Room, and the name stuck.

I added to the ambiance by posting pictures related to the pleasure of reading, some clipped from magazines and many copied from a book of photographs taken by André Kertész (1971). I also displayed photographs I took of the students reading and drawings they made of special places they liked to read at home. Children were immersed in many images of a reading life!

To set up a reading nook in your classroom, first find a quiet corner or a secluded spot away from traffic (Figure 6.5). Furnish the nook with comfortable, child-size seating (beanbag chairs, mini couches or easy chairs, a yoga mat, pillows, carpeting squares), and a small lamp. Invite children to help make the space their own by drawing pictures, making signs, or taking photographs

Figure 6.4. Children worked together to design and set up this book nook.

Figure 6.5. A reading nook with a curtain

to go on the walls. A filmy curtain makes the area more private, and you might include a few stuffed animals for children to cuddle with or read to. I once saw Enid, a quiet, shy child, very seriously reading a book to a stuffed bunny rabbit, carefully showing the illustration before turning each page. It's also helpful to have a variety of tools readers might use in the space, such as sticky notes, pencils for taking notes, pointers, and bookmarks.

Children can certainly bring books with them when they visit the reading nook, but it's also a good idea to have some books stored in the space and on display. A small bookshelf or display rack will work, as well as baskets or bins for books. In my classroom, we decided each week at a class meeting which books to include in the nook. The decision was influenced by what the class was currently studying. For example, if we were learning about folktales, the children wanted to have lots of favorite folktales there. If the class was engaged in emergent storybook reading (Sulzby 1971), then I had a basket of emergent storybooks, such as *Caps for Sale* (Esphyr Slobodkina) and *Blueberries for Sal* (Robert McCloskey). Also, be sure to include favorite books you have read aloud. In *Read to Me: Raising Kids Who Love to Read*, Bea Cullinan writes, "Children want to read on their own the books they've heard read aloud" (2007, 47).

Establishing Management Guidelines

For children to feel like they really own the space, they should help make the rules for the reading nook, although you will be an important facilitator. Things to discuss and decide with children include the following:

- How many children can use the book nook at one time?
- How should readers behave in the book nook? Requiring children to be seated as they read or have conversations keeps the nook from becoming a playroom. You might also discuss appropriate voice levels: what does quiet (not necessarily silent) reading sound like? You should also reiterate and model the proper behavior for sharing a book with a partner.
- What is the proper way to handle books? For example, it's not OK for books to be strewn on the floor.
- How many books can be brought from the class library to the book nook at one time? When will they be returned?
- Will class monitors organize the book nook?

- Who will decide what books will be included in the center each week? When? On Friday afternoon so the books will be there on Monday morning?
- Who will bring the books to the nook? You? The class library monitor?
- Will there be a theme (fairy tales, bridges, winter, dinosaurs, etc.) each week or month?

Launching the Reading Nook

Because most children are familiar with books when they come to school (or will be after a few days in a classroom), launching the reading nook as a free-choice activity is fairly easy compared with launching other centers with more involved materials and activities. There are lots of ways you might introduce the nook, but whatever you decide, it should probably include some discussion of how people enjoy reading in the world.

In *The Art of Teaching Reading* (2000), Lucy Calkins tells how Kathy Collins began the year in her first-grade classroom by inviting children to bring in their favorite books as a way to jump-start conversations about the importance of reading in their lives. Children shared stories about reading in bed with their parents and waiting for younger siblings to go to sleep before their mom or dad could read to them. One child talked about how her grandmother read the Bible to her and used a scrap of paper as a bookmark. By inviting children to share stories about their private reading lives, we let children know we value their reading choices. A discussion about students' private reading lives is a wonderful segue into setting up a comfortable reading corner in the classroom and offering it as a free-choice option.

Children will also need to understand that when they choose to visit the reading nook, they also get to choose the books they want to read (see Figure 6.6). This is different from reading workshop, where they read books at their instructional level (just-right books). Free book choice is important because personal interests and independent reading levels don't always coincide. A child obsessed with the Brooklyn Bridge might not find books on this topic that he can both decode and comprehend. However, in the reading nook he can look at

Figure 6.6. A child chooses her own books.

the pictures in a beautiful nonfiction book about bridges and study the diagrams and maps. Kathy Collins and Matt Glover write that educators need to "instill the habits of mind of being curious, wondering, asking questions, developing interests, clearing up confusions, sharing knowledge, and so much more" (2015, 78). Giving children the opportunity to read and better yet enjoy books that support their interests sends a powerful message about the importance of books and reading in their lives.

Spotlight on Inquiry-Driven Centers

Inquiry projects sometimes happen in the most serendipitous ways.

Once, after visiting London during a school vacation, I brought back postcards of different sights to share with the children in my kindergarten class. When I shared a reproduction of the Rosetta stone, three boys asked me if they could look at it during choice time. They sat with magnifying glasses, looking closely at the picture, and became both excited and curious when they discovered the hieroglyphic images. *What do these mean? Why are they here?*

More children walked over to see what was causing all of the excitement at this new center. As I observed, I remembered that I had a hieroglyphic ABC chart stuffed somewhere in my supply closet. I found it and brought it to the table. The children were eager to decipher some of what was written on the stone.

The boys asked to stay at this center the next day because they had a great idea that they wanted to keep secret. They said they would need a large sheet of paper, glue, markers, and some more paper. I wondered what they were going to do but made sure that they had all that they needed for their secret project.

The next day the three boys began working on a name chart. They folded a piece of paper, wrote a classmate's name on the inside, and on the outside of the fold they wrote the name in hieroglyphs. When they shared the name chart at the end of the week, the children asked if we could all find out more about ancient Egypt.

The children's interest provoked a class trip to the library to find books about the topic and to the Brooklyn Museum to see the Egyptian collection. There was a flurry of new center activity. Some children built pyramids with blocks using pictures from a book about ancient Egypt to guide them. (There were many block crashes those two weeks!) Others used the computer to find new information about ancient Egypt that they recorded on cards and then illustrated. Another group of children used papier-mâché to create a life-size sarcophagus and made up a story about a person who was buried there. When the sarcophagus was completed and dry, the whole class went to the schoolyard to spray it with gold paint. The storywriters "translated" their story onto strips of paper using the hieroglyphic ABC chart and glued it onto the sarcophagus. (See Figures 6.7 and 6.8.)

This was a short, unexpected kindergarten study driven completely by children's interest and energy.

Figure 6.7. Children working together on the sarcophagus

Figure 6.8. The finished sarcophagus

Enhancing and Enriching the Reading Nook

Once children have some experience with the reading nook and are comfortable choosing it, you can consider enhancing and enriching the space in ways that match the interests of your students. There are many possibilities—basically anything connected to readers and reading might happen in the nook.

Utilize Author-Themed and Topic-Themed Baskets

One addition you might make is to encourage children to create baskets of books for authors and topics. I happened upon the power of this enrichment quite fortunately one year when I noticed that Benjamin consistently read Dr. Seuss books, which were scattered among our not-yet-labeled book baskets. At a class meeting, I said I'd noticed how much Benjamin loved Dr. Seuss books and wondered what about them he found so interesting. Hands flew up, and students offered their opinions. "They are so funny" was the most popular response. Benjamin added, "Yes, and I love the pictures. They're really silly!"

I confided, "Benjamin and I are very much alike. When I like a book, I search out other books written by the same author and read them again and again. Last summer I read three books by Isabel Allende, and at the end of the summer I read the first book again. I keep all my Isabel Allende books together on a shelf so I can find them easily. Do any of you do the same thing?"

I then gave Benjamin a basket for his Dr. Seuss books, which he could bring to the reading nook, and suggested that his classmates add any Dr. Seuss books to the basket if they found them in the library. This triggered a flurry of activity. Children found Dr. Seuss books and put them in Benjamin's basket. They also began creating their own baskets of books by favorite authors—Donald Crews, Margaret Wise Brown, Maurice Sendak, Eric Carle. Children asked, "I really like pop-up books. Can I make a pop-up book basket?" and "Can I have a basket about cats? I want to read a lot about cats because my mommy said that we can get a kitten soon." But something else was happening as well: children were learning about one another's interests. They borrowed baskets to bring to the reading nook and said things like "I'm going to read lots of Eric Carle books today just like Evelyn."

Create a Book-Sharing Board

Adding a book-sharing corkboard to the reading nook gives children a space where they can post information about books they particularly enjoyed reading. Young children could draw a favorite illustration from the book on card stock and pin it on the board. Children in first and second grade might be more specific: "I loved *Where the Wild Things Are* because it made me feel like I'm living in a forest with Max. I loved when Max stared at the monsters!" Children might also use the space to recommend books to each other: "I think that Sammy would love reading *Nate the Great* because Sammy likes to solve mysteries and so does Nate." These short book shares reinforce that your classroom is a community of readers who all have reading personalities.

Add Tools That Support Engagement

Adding simple tools can deepen children's interest in the reading nook. For example, just before Halloween one year, when children were filled with the excitement of the holiday, I introduced the big book *In a Dark, Dark Room* (Alvin Schwartz) for shared reading. I turned off the classroom lights and used a flashlight to point to each word as the children read along with me. On subsequent days that week, I let various children use the flashlight pointer as we read. The next week, after discussing how to handle a flashlight safely (Never point it at your or your friend's eyes), I added a tiny flashlight to the reading nook. The children loved bringing big books to the nook and taking turns illuminating the text as they read. Highlighting each word as they told the story was a particularly powerful experience for children who were just starting to focus on decoding print.

Invite Students to Make New Jackets for Favorite Books

A later-in-the-year activity children love is making new book jackets for favorite books. When you introduce a new book, always examine the book jacket—the illustration, the blurbs about the book, the short summary on the front inside flap, and the information about the author on the back inside flap. Invite the children who elect to spend time in the reading nook several days in a row to pick a favorite book and make a new jacket for the book:

1. Encourage the children to reread the book and talk about it. (Join in if you wish.)
2. Help them fold a large piece of paper (the paper in an easel pad works well) into the form of a book cover.
3. Suggest that they create a new illustration for the cover based on what they think is most important about the book.
4. Remind them to include the title, the author's name, and the names of the illustrators (the original illustrator's name and their name, since they created the new cover).
5. Suggest that they write a few sentences describing the story or theme of the book on the front inside flap.
6. Ask them to write something about themselves (their name, age, interests, etc.) on the back inside flap.
7. Return the books, with the new jackets in place, to the library or reading nook basket.
8. Later, you might remove the book jackets and display them in the reading nook.

Take Advantage of Unexpected Opportunities

If you pay attention to children who enjoy visiting the reading nook, you will often see unexpected possibilities for enrichment in their play. For example, Bill Fulbrecht noticed that his kindergartners who came to the reading nook were putting books in piles, stacking the piles at the entrance, and inviting other children to stop by and browse. They told Bill they were running a bookstore. Bill wondered whether this interest would stick or fizzle out. Not only did it continue, but more and more children began stopping by the impromptu bookstore. At a class meeting, Bill asked the children what they knew about bookstores and what they would like to learn about them. They took a field trip to a local bookstore, and when they returned, they decided to build a big bookstore in the block center. They worked on this for days, even constructing a conveyor belt and a small café in imitation of what they'd seen at the real bookstore. They moved books into their new bookstore and played bookstore for the next two weeks. When their interest waned, they took the bookstore down, and the block center was home to new constructions.

Here's the trajectory this enhancement took:

- Bill noticed what the children were doing and asked questions that helped them self-reflect. Their answers clued him in to their thoughts and actions.
- He observed for a few days to see whether the activity was sustainable.
- He shared his observations with the class, opening a discussion.
- He arranged a field trip to a bookstore to give the children a common experience.
- He allowed children to combine centers, thus broadening and integrating their learning experience.
- He recognized when the students lost interest and it was time to move on.

When your students develop a particular interest in the reading nook, support it! Offering a few key supports (a class discussion about how the center might change to support their interest, a field trip, new materials, etc.) can extend and enrich the children's experience.

Observing to Learn

The reading nook is a choice activity and a place for playful explorations and learning centered on books and conversation related to children's independent reading. When you observe children in the reading nook, you tap into a rich resource for understanding their reading interests, their natural reading behaviors and preferences, and their challenges. Focused observations help you plan more intentionally for everything from partnerships to genre and inquiry studies in reading and writing workshop. Does Manny like to read alone? Is José a social reader? Are the children obsessed with books about bridges? Trains? Have they lost interest in fairy tales?

Observations also help you assess to what extent your teaching in reading workshop is taking hold in children's independent reading. Children will show you what they've mastered and what needs more time and teaching. Following are some behaviors you might look for:

- Using reading strategies explicitly taught during reading workshop
  - rereading for comprehension
  - making connections between the illustrations and the print
  - exhibiting appropriate book-handling skills (for the youngest readers, holding the book correctly with the cover in the front and turning pages from front to back)
  - selecting books that are a good fit
- Being good reading partners
  - sitting shoulder to shoulder
  - holding the book so both readers can see
  - preparing a plan for reading together (choral reading or "you read a page and then I read a page")
  - stopping to talk about what they have read
- Following an interest or a passion in reading
- Using reading tools introduced in reading workshop
  - sticky notes
  - pointers
  - finger pointing (beginning readers)
  - bookmarks

Figure 6.9. Children reading together about a topic that interests them

As you assess and observe children in the reading nook, you'll need to decide when to stand back and observe and when to step in with questions and suggestions. The goal is to support children in thoughtful ways but not make them feel like they are being evaluated and censured as readers. When in doubt, remember that you can always address any issue you observe with teaching during reading workshop so you preserve children's feeling of independence while they're in the reading nook.

Teaching Interventions in the Reading Nook

In the reading nook, as in any center, it's not unusual for problems to arise that will need your attention. The Teaching Interventions show some common scenarios with suggested interventions that will help children develop as independent readers.

Teaching Interventions

Observation	Possible Response
Mary and Max are bringing more books into the reading nook. The books already there are scattered haphazardly on the floor.	Ask the children whether they have considered which books fit their reading plan. Suggest they have a discussion to decide how many books they need.
Sydney and Sara are reading alternate pages, but it is obvious from the position of the book on Sydney's lap that Sara is having difficulty seeing the page.	You might ask the children to make a plan for how they will hold the book as they're reading. Have them decide if they will take turns reading pages or read together like a chorus.
Karen and Joshua want to read together but are arguing about what book to read.	Compliment them on their decision to read together and acknowledge their difficulty. Let them know this happens to lots of readers who read together. Suggest they make a plan for sharing book choices, perhaps taking turns, as many people in book clubs do.
Erika has chosen the reading nook even though nobody else has, and you're afraid she may not remain engaged for the full period. When you stop by, she is animatedly reading a book to a teddy bear.	Ask Erika if you can listen as she reads to the teddy bear. After hearing some of the story, ask whether she would like to share the story in a class meeting. If she seems interested but reluctant, suggest that you read the story together instead, alternating pages.

continues

Observation	Possible Response
Children are playing in a way that isn't appropriate—climbing on chairs, tossing pillows, and so on. Eliminating the reading nook is tempting, but that also eliminates a valuable free-choice option.	Scolding has no long-term benefits. Instead, discuss the problem. Did the children pick the reading nook even though it didn't really interest them? Are they clear about how the reading nook should be used? Then redirect. What books would interest them? Give them an empty basket and suggest they look through the classroom library for a few books they would like to read that day. Or suggest they create a poster describing how to use the reading nook and post it there.

If an intervention works particularly well for students, it's always a good idea to share it with the rest of the class during a class meeting. You might also provide a bulletin board where children can share their strategies for solving reading nook problems. The goal, of course, is to help children enjoy the center and also develop independence as readers and problem solvers.

> When children pretend, they're using their imaginations to move beyond the bounds of reality. A stick can be a magic wand. A sock can be a puppet. A small child can be a superhero.
>
> —**Fred Rogers** ("Mr. Rogers")

Dramatic Play Center

Evelyn and Jeff have turned our "pretend" center into a doctor's office. They've covered the play stove with white paper to become the examining table. Placing her baby doll on the table, Evelyn, dressed up in silver high heels and my daughter's outgrown fancy party dress, pretends to cry. "My baby is dead," she sobs as Jeff, the "doctor," dressed in an oversized white shirt with a stethoscope dangling from his neck, takes rapid "notes" on a pad.

He says, "Don't worry; I'll fix the baby." He takes a needle from the play doctor's kit and jabs the baby doll's arm. "OK, now. The baby's not dead anymore." Evelyn picks up her baby, hands over a wad of play money from the pocketbook draped over her shoulder, and happily teeters away on her high-heeled shoes.

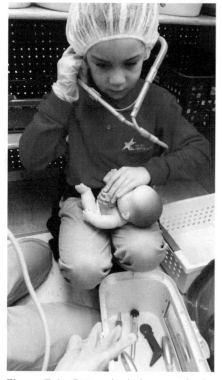

Figure 7.1. Giving the baby a medical checkup is serious business in the dramatic play center.

Watching children at dramatic play is a little like watching a production of a play by Samuel Beckett, an originator of Theatre of the Absurd. Things look slightly "right," but "wrong" enough to tilt life as we know it on its side. In the dramatic play described above, Evelyn understands that one brings a sick baby to the doctor. However, she and Jeff misunderstand the finality of death and the powers of the medical profession: the doctor magically brings the baby back to life. They solve their problem in a way consistent with children's knowledge of the human life cycle and their trust in the power of doctors. Vivian Gussin Paley refers to this type of play, in which the dead can be instantly resurrected, as *magical play*. In *Boys and Girls: Superheroes in the Doll Corner*, she writes, "The same magic destroys and resurrects, creates an orphan or mother—or the Green Slime. The ability to *imagine* something is the magic; putting it into action is the play; playing it out is the safe way to discharge the idea" (1984, 80).

When we give children the freedom to use objects and materials as they wish, we empower them to dig deep into their imagination and draw on the experiences of their individual and collective lives. They might transform a large carton into a house or a spaceship. A folded square of paper becomes a handy road map as they sit in lined-up chairs (a car!), driving toward a vacation in the country. Flowing strips of fabric become a queen's dress, and a decorated chair is the throne that awaits her. A. A. Milne perfectly expresses the magic of this sort of pretend play in *Winnie-the-Pooh*:

> "Hallo, Rabbit," [Pooh] said, "is that you?"
> "Let's pretend it isn't," said Rabbit, "and see what happens." (1957, 106)

Children engage in dramatic play with a "let's see what happens" sense of possibility and have free rein to express and interpret their knowledge and understanding of the adult world. As they play, they synthesize past experience and demonstrate their understanding of acceptable social relationships, revealing their interests and confusions. When they improvise roles and situations, they foster the cognitive thinking that supports learning to read, write stories, and understand the complexities of mathematics. Russian psychologist Lev Vygotsky wrote that "play contains all developmental tendencies in a condensed form and is itself a major source of development" (1978, 102).

In a single episode of dramatic play, so much rich learning happens. For example, children acting out a narrative are having experiences they may reuse when they create narratives in their writing. They develop a background that supports their understanding of texts and their ability to predict what will happen next in a story. By making signs for a restaurant, doctor's office, or post office, they begin to understand the function of print in the environment. Rearranging furnishings to create a store, a hospital, or a space station develops an understanding of spatial relationships. Setting a table for a pretend meal involves counting and matching. The writer and naturalist Diane Ackerman contends that "play is our brain's favorite way of learning" (2000, 11), a truth on display each moment children are engaged in a dramatic play center.

Figure 7.2. Students designed, set up, and labeled an emergency room.

Setting Up a Dramatic Play Center

Anyone who's spent much time around young children knows that it doesn't take much to encourage dramatic play. Even the simplest objects are quickly transformed in the hands of imaginative children. Knowing this, we realize the possibilities for a dramatic play center are virtually limitless. So where do you even start?

It makes sense to first consider the age of the children you will be teaching. At the beginning of the school year a dramatic play center in prekindergarten and kindergarten often resembles a kitchen and may include a baby bed with

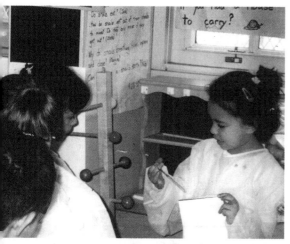

Figure 7.3. The dramatic play center as a doctor's office

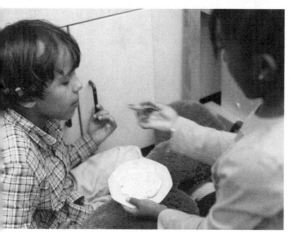

Figure 7.4. The dramatic play center as a restaurant

blankets, dolls, and stuffed animals. This familiar configuration is important because it helps young children make the transition from home to a new, unfamiliar classroom. Later in the year, the center can transform into any sort of place the children might imagine—a doctor's office, a post office, a bookstore, a restaurant (see Figures 7.3 and 7.4).

First and second graders are still young children who love to pretend, but their classrooms may not have a formally designated, furnished area for dramatic play. If this is the case in your classroom, consider creating baskets of props children can use imaginatively in any open space to improvise interactions. You might begin the year with a variety of props, for example, different fabrics for creating costumes, play dishes, a doll or two, perhaps a stethoscope, a tape measure, or a magnifying glass. As children play with the props, they'll no doubt suggest others to add, and as the year progresses, you can tailor prop baskets to reflect particular interests the children have, a class inquiry, or a read-aloud.

Space and Location

The first decision you will have to make is whether or not you will have a dedicated space in the classroom for dramatic play. If the answer is yes, then the next decision is where to locate it. It's important to remember that this is a very active center, particularly in prekindergarten and kindergarten. If the area is too small, the possibilities are limited and children get in one another's way. There needs to be enough space for productive, interactive play where children can engage in conversations and movements without disturbing quieter areas of the classroom. It's best if the center is located where it won't interfere with classroom traffic.

If you are open to allowing interactions between the children in the dramatic play center and other centers in the room, then it's also helpful to think about the center's proximity to other areas. There are logical opportunities for interaction between the block center and the dramatic play center, and positioning them next to each other encourages interesting interchanges. For example, one day when my kindergartners were in the middle of a bridge study, I noticed dishes and silverware in the block center. Annoyed by the mess, I investigated and discovered that the children in the dramatic play center were playing restaurant and had decided to bring coffee and cake to the workers next door, who were building a bridge. This interaction raised the level of the children's conversations and revealed their understanding of coffee breaks and restaurant deliveries in the outside world.

In fact, dramatic play often spills out into other areas of the room for all kinds of reasons, so remember that even when you designate a space for the center, its boundaries are often negotiable. I once had a group of children in the dramatic play center who decided to pretend they were going to the beach. They left the center, and our meeting carpet became the seaside, where they spread out blankets and set up a picnic. When they asked for a beach ball to play with, I hesitated but decided to give them a small rubber ball. I reminded them that the "beach ball" needed to stay on the "sand" and walked away, trusting that they would make sure it did. My confidence in their highly serious play overrode the rule about not throwing a ball around the classroom.

If you determine you don't have enough room for a permanent dramatic play center, then the best alternative is to create prop boxes that can be used in any open space. My friend Bill Fulbrecht felt there wasn't enough space in his classroom for both a block center and a dramatic play center, so he sent all the dramatic play furniture to a school storage room. Then he searched the other classrooms for large hollow wooden blocks that weren't being used. He put a low, curtained bookshelf next to the meeting area carpet to hold the hollow blocks and baskets of props so the meeting area could also be used for dramatic play (see Figure 7.5).

Figure 7.5. Locating dramatic play materials near the meeting carpet with hollow blocks leaves more space for a large block center.

Spotlight on Inquiry-Driven Centers

A first-grade class was engaged in a study of the emergency room at a local hospital. Many of the children's families often used this facility for nonemergency visits rather than visiting a private doctor. During choice time, children re-created the emergency room in the block corner. The children first worked together to draw a blueprint of a waiting room with different spaces appropriate for mothers with new babies, toddlers, children their age, and teenagers, and one for grandpas and grandmas. They then built it using Legos. The science and art center were combined as children created a life-size human skeleton, using the overhead projector to study X-rays.

Some of the children asked if they could make a doctor's office where they could play "hospital." The teacher rearranged some of the classroom furniture and made room for a dramatic play center. The children used sketches and photographs from a class visit to the emergency room to guide them as they created this office. They labeled recycled bottles to make medicine containers, they covered a table with white paper to make an examining table, and they borrowed dolls from the kindergarten class to serve as patients.

Then something quite unexpected happened. The children in the hospital area periodically rushed across the room to the children at the science center so their babies could be x-rayed. They were then given prescriptions to bring back to their hospital so the babies' broken bones could be repaired.

This was a class of mostly ELL children, and through this hospital dramatic play they were using their new vocabulary, drawing on their trip experiences, collaborating in their dramatic play, using writing to communicate ideas, creating, innovating, and imagining!

Furnishings, Costumes, and Props

In many classrooms, a dramatic play center is furnished with a commercially purchased sink, stove, refrigerator, and hutch or cabinet. However, referring to the space as the housekeeping center limits the possibilities: children's dramatic play need not be tied to the home. Children can be quite creative in transforming these pieces of furniture into anything they can imagine. For example, cover the stove with white paper and it becomes an examining table in a veterinarian's office or a hospital. An ironing board can easily double as a receptionist's desk in a business office, or a hutch or cabinet as a waiter's station in a restaurant. You might consider including large hollow wooden blocks in addition to (or instead of) traditional play furniture to give children more control over their play. Blocks or even large empty boxes can be easily transformed to create places like a theatre, an airplane, or a pizzeria with an oven, tables, and a counter (see Figure 7.6). And last but not least, children love to look at their reflections, particularly when they are transforming themselves

Figure 7.6. Children made a fort in Wendy Sawyer's kindergarten class.

with costumes, so a full-length unbreakable mirror is a valuable addition to the center (reflective Mylar is a good alternative).

As with any center, overloading the dramatic play area with too many props may overwhelm the children, and they might use them less thoughtfully. At the beginning of the year, it's best to start with props that are familiar to children from their lives outside school. Here are some basics you might consider:

- plastic dishes, cups, and utensils; a pot or pan; and a tablecloth
- a child-size broom, dustpan, and mop
- dress-up clothes appropriate for both boys and girls (Be sure there are hangers, hooks, and baskets to contain them. Begin the year with just a few until children understand how to care for them.)
- various kinds of fabric that children can use to create their own costumes (You'll be surprised and delighted by what they come up with!)
- dolls, a crib or bed, doll clothes, and small blankets
- wallets and purses
- keys on key chains
- a telephone, perhaps some old cell phones, and an old telephone directory
- notepads and writing utensils
- a small suitcase and an attaché case.

As the year progresses, you'll want to add new props to the center and retire others to reflect the interests of your students and the twists and turns in your curriculum. Invite the children to suggest props they'd like to have in the center and write their suggestions on a chart. They may be able to make some of the items in the art center and create appropriate signs and posters in the writing center. You can also ask them to help you write a letter to families and staff asking for donations.

The key to keeping children's engagement with the center alive and active is paying attention to their play and making sure the center supports their interests. For example, practically every group of children I've ever taught have, at one time or another, played restaurant in the dramatic play center. When you see a particular interest like this, it's easy to encourage more detailed and realistic play scenarios by discussing restaurant experiences during class meetings, reading aloud books about restaurants, and if possible visiting a local restaurant. Then, make sure the props in the center support the interest as well. For children to play restaurant, you might include the following:

- aprons
- menus, placemats, Open and Closed signs, and a sign listing the hours of operation (These could be created in the writing center.)
- play food
- tablecloths and napkins
- a whiteboard for listing daily specials
- order pads
- trays (The school lunchroom is a possible source.)
- a basket of cookbooks and other books about restaurants.

Sometimes a class inquiry will lend itself naturally to dramatic play and you will shift the props once again to support this play. For example, the center might become a firehouse in connection with a field trip to a firehouse. You can provide flashlights, plastic fire hats, plastic hoses, gloves, rubber boots, books about firehouses, and photographs of firefighters and firehouses. The children might also create their own props in the art center—a firefighter's axe, for example. I've seen children tape together the cardboard tubes from paper towel rolls and paint them to look like the pole firefighters slide down.

Organization and Management

One of the first decisions you will have to make is how many children can play in the center at one time. You'll consider the size of the space and the number of props, and you might ask children for their input about a "just right" number. The thinking they will do as they consider this question may help them be more thoughtful and intentional about their play in the center.

Because dramatic play is entirely child initiated, conflicts aren't unusual, often with regard to roles: *I want to be the doctor. No,* I'm *going to be the doctor!* When conflicts arise, it's important not to intervene unless it's absolutely necessary. Remember that children are learning to negotiate different social territories through their dramatic play, and they can't do that if adults are always stepping in to fix things. Children are often better at solving their disputes than we think they will be, and it's what we want them to learn to do. If you see that children do work a conflict out themselves, their problem and solution would be perfect for sharing in a class meeting. Of course, sometimes all children need is a gentle reminder that by spending so much time arguing, they are losing play time.

Another management issue is cleanup. Dress-up clothes, dishes, and dolls will no doubt get scattered around while children are playing. If children are responsible for cleaning up the center, it's important to prepare clearly marked and easily accessible places for all the props and make it clear they should be returned there at the end of playtime. If you see that children aren't cleaning up the center properly, consider raising the issue during a class meeting. Let the children be problem solvers and contribute their own ideas and suggestions. The guidelines they arrive at for themselves will be much more powerful and meaningful.

As mentioned earlier, dramatic play also tends to spill into other areas in the room. If there's a baby carriage, for example, students will almost certainly wheel it around the room on a "walk." If you're uncomfortable with children playing outside their centers, one way to head off this management problem is to remove props that suggest a range of movement, as a carriage does. But you might also discuss movement with the children and come up with guidelines for when they can and can't take their play outside the boundaries of the center.

Launching the Dramatic Play Center

The dramatic play center is very easy to get up and running at the beginning of prekindergarten or kindergarten because the children are eager to play and naturally know how to engage with props. If the center is appealingly arranged, has enough room to move around, and contains interesting props, children can move right in and get started without an introductory minilesson. First or second graders can get started right away too, but you might also wait until your students have had some common experiences to fuel their play. Reading engaging stories aloud or beginning a social studies investigation will give them lots of ideas, and you can provide prop boxes to support those ideas.

Enhancing and Enriching the Dramatic Play Center

Observe how children interact with one another, the language they use, and how they improvise with the props and materials in dramatic play to get a sense of their thinking and learning and generate ideas for creating rich and meaningful curriculum. Dramatic play reflects children's free and creative interpretation of what they have experienced and know about both real and storybook life.

Initiate a Class Discussion

The simplest way to enhance and enrich the center is to talk with children about what you've observed in their dramatic play and help them imagine new possibilities. For example, if you've noticed children talking on the telephone a lot in the center, at the next class meeting, say, "I noticed lots of conversations on the telephone. What might we add to the telephone table? Do you have any ideas about what you might need to find telephone numbers? How about remembering your messages? Let's see if we can come up with a list of some new things that we can bring in for the telephone table." When you invite children to plan for their play, you help them become much more intentional when they're actually engaged in that play.

Introduce a Class Ministudy

One year I observed a lot of children pretending to be kings and queens. I mentioned this at a class meeting, which led to an enthusiastic discussion about kings, queens, and castles. To build on this enthusiasm, I read aloud several versions of the Cinderella story. In our school library I found some nonfiction books about castles, including David Macaulay's wonderfully descriptive *Castle*, and gathered them in a book bin labeled "Books About Castles, Kings, and Queens." The big book *The King's Cake*, by Jill Eggleton, was that week's shared reading. The children's interest snowballed. They built castles, moats included, in the block area. We visited a castle-like church in upper Manhattan, the Cathedral Church of Saint John the Divine. Our former student teacher, who was interning as a tour guide there, gave child-friendly explanations of the various architectural features. The children were particularly fascinated by the rose windows and the flying buttresses. Back at school, the children in the art center made tie-dyed rose windows for their pretend castle. They transformed two chairs into thrones and made crowns to wear. A class ministudy was born.

There are some important steps to take before turning the dramatic play area into a larger class ministudy:

- Observe children over several days and write down your observations and bits of conversation.
- Don't jump into a study. Wait. See if a particular interest continues.
- Share your observations in a class discussion.
- Gauge children's interest and enthusiasm.
- If there is a lot of enthusiasm, plant the idea that they might want to learn more about the topic and then equip the dramatic play center accordingly.
- Map out possibilities: materials you would need, possible trips, books, cross-curricular opportunities for learning, questions children might have, ways to address the standards, and opportunities to embed reading and writing. (You won't cover everything, of course, but this will help you plan and prepare.)
- Allow some time for the idea to percolate. Ask the children to talk with one another and their families about it and share their ideas and suggestions the next day.
- If the children return the next day still filled with enthusiasm, you're ready to go!

Add Prop Boxes

Around midyear, it is not unusual for winter doldrums to set in, especially if ice and freezing weather have prevented playing outdoors. Your students (and you!) might be getting edgy and need something new and exciting. Adding prop boxes for dramatic play could be the answer.

First, invite children to brainstorm a number of play scenarios and record their ideas, and then prepare a box for each scenario filled with related props. You may already have some of the materials, but you might also need to borrow from other classrooms, ask children to bring materials from home, or have them make props in the art center. Then have children label each box and decorate the outside to reflect what's inside.

Be forewarned that prop boxes often introduce new management issues in the dramatic play area. If four children choose the center, they all need to agree on which box to open and play with. To head off this tricky problem, you might role-play choosing a prop box in a class meeting. In the discussion around the role-playing, encourage children to come up with some simple rules for dealing with conflict when making choices about prop boxes.

Incorporate Literacy and Mathematics

Incorporating opportunities for children to use reading, writing, and math in their dramatic play is really quite easy and is the perfect way to enhance and enrich children's learning in the center. There are many possibilities.

Literacy

- Be sure there are notepads, sticky notes, and writing implements in the center.
- Include a variety of pencils, pens, and markers.
- Create a class telephone directory, with a picture of each child and his or her phone number and address. Put it next to a play telephone, along with a notepad for taking phone messages.
- Encourage children to create appropriate signs.
- Add magazines. Children often see their parents and caregivers reading magazines.
- Provide a basket of appropriate books.
- Include maps; they add an extra dimension to "going on a trip."
- Add a clipboard and charts in a doctor's office for recording patient information (see Figure 7.7).
- Add cancelled stamps, a magnifying glass, blank paper for making stamps and envelopes, and a hanging shoe organizer (use the pockets as mailboxes) in a post office.

Figure 7.7. A child takes notes in the dramatic play center, which has become a doctor's office.

- Include walkie-talkies and telephones to support language development.
- Provide circulars and coupons in a supermarket.

Mathematics

- Add a balance scale to the center, particularly if the children are playing supermarket. (Demonstrate how it works beforehand.)
- Add a cash register and play money if the children are playing store or restaurant.
- Provide a tape measure (perhaps taped to the wall, as many parents do at home to track a child's growth).
- Add a scale in a doctor's office.

Observing to Learn

Because children's dramatic play can take them anywhere their imaginations lead, your observation of children in the center is likely to yield insights about a wide range of development. Because of this, you'll need a wider lens to view children in dramatic play than you use in a more targeted area like the reading nook or science center. At a conference presentation in Reggio Emilia, I was introduced to a practical and easy template for observing children. The tool is helpful when observing children in any situation, but particularly so in dramatic play. For example, the next page shows a chart a teacher filled out after observing the children from this chapter's opening vignette.

It takes only a few minutes to jot down an observation and a brief transcript of what children are saying as they play. You can reflect on these observations during a prep period or after the children have gone home as you plan your next steps. You can also share this form during grade-level meetings. Discussing your reflections and planning next steps with your colleagues will help you interpret children's actions and language and prompt interesting discussions on the importance of dramatic play.

Date: 1/14/ 2009

Center: Dramatic Play (Doctor's Office)

Children: Evelyn, Jeff, Matthew

The three children are English language learners. J. speaks Creole at home; E. and M. speak Spanish as a first language.

Observations	Reflections on the Observations	Next Steps
E. is dressed up in play clothes and is trying to balance herself on high heels. J. is wearing a white shirt and has a stethoscope hanging from his neck.	Piaget referred to language as a verbal way of expressing an understanding of the world.	When M. is at his next center, I'm going to join his group and help him enter the conversation.
E. brings her doll to J. and says, "My baby is dead." She is pretending to sob. J. seems to be writing notes on a pad.	Even though E. and J. had a limited grasp of English, they were able to use enough to show their understanding of the problem.	I also wonder if I need to have some small-group discussions with my ELL students—perhaps reading aloud a previously read book, talking about it, and acting it out. That will give me an opportunity to model a few helpful expressions and give the children the opportunity to practice them in small groups with my support.
J. tells E. that he will fix the baby and jabs the doll with a pretend injection. J.: "OK, now. The baby's not dead anymore."	M. was silent. I'm wondering if it's shyness or his inability to express himself. Because of his lack of participation, I can't determine what he understands.	
M. is uninvolved, watching the interaction between J. and E.		

Teaching Interventions in the Dramatic Play Center

As mentioned earlier, problems are certain to arise as children are at play in the center, and for the most part, you want to hang back and let children work them out on their own. When you do decide to intervene, it's important to be thoughtful about *how* you are offering assistance. It's helpful to ask open-ended questions or model a strategy that will scaffold the children's play, but the goal is not to provide a script or to direct the play. The range of issues children might encounter is wide, but the chart of teaching interventions presents a couple of examples to give you a feel for sensible interventions. Notice how each one incorporates even more dramatic play into the problem solving.

Teaching Interventions

Observation	Possible Response
A child persists in crawling around the center while barking like a dog, to the consternation of the other children.	Add some direction to the child's play and involve the other children by asking, "I wonder what the family will need to do to care for their puppy?" Provide drawing paper and crayons or pencils so the children can draw pictures of what the puppy will need and what they will need to do to take care of the puppy.
Baby dolls are strewn about on the floor of the center.	Pick up a doll, put it in your lap, and ask, "What do you know about how we need to care for babies?" List children's responses on a chart—just a few words, along with simple drawings. "Now I'm going to tape up your wonderful ideas for taking care of babies for you to see because you know so much about caring for your babies. Let's pick them all up now so we can take care of them." Something else to consider: having too many dolls in the center can lead to children's indifference.

8

> With me,
> everything turns
> into mathematics.
>
> —René Descartes

Math Center

A group of kindergartners in the math center place a bin of Unifix cubes in the middle of the table. Although they are working in pairs, all the pairs are creating rods of ten.

Michael asks, "How do I do this?"

David responds, "Use yellow and purple. No! This doesn't go here!" Michael takes away a blue cube that David has attached to one of the yellow cubes. David counts as he places nine yellow Unfix cubes out on the table, and then Michael attaches one more purple cube to the line of yellow ones.

Jeremy says to Jenay, "You put five red and---" but she interrupts him to explain it her own way.

"Put five red and count the blue to 10—6, 7, 8, 9, 10. See?" she says.

At the other end of the table, George takes some blue and yellow cubes and begins alternating one blue cube and one yellow cube until his partner Ted stops him. "Don't make a pattern. Use all the blue first and then yellow." They work together to connect six blue cubes. Then Ted says, "And now five yellow." He adds five yellow cubes, and they count the cubes together. George realizes they have too many and he removes a yellow cube as they begin counting them together again.

It's early in the year and these six children are just beginning to explore ideas together in the math center, but already they are engaging in "the most important kind of language children can learn in a stimulating mathematics program . . . the language of thinking, justification, and proof" (Lee and Ginsberg 2009, 40). In the math center, children make their own decisions about what math materials to use and how to use them. They can create aesthetically pleasing patterns, practice mathematically challenging games, and use their knowledge of mathematics to design their own games and activities. Over time, this freedom of exploration supports children in several ways:

- They learn to talk about their own thinking (*I added by counting them all up on my fingers.*).
- They learn to justify their answers (*I knew it was a triangle because I saw that it had three sides.*) and propose proofs (*This can't be a circle; it only has straight lines.*).
- They practice verbal communication about math concepts, something more important than remembering facts.

They are also, of course, learning important skills. Mathematical skills are necessary in all aspects of adult life, not only in technology, science, or engineering, but wherever analytical thinking is required (Duncan et al. 2007). The National Council of Teachers of Mathematics describes three important qualities of good mathematics programs for children in preK through grade 2. Through a program, children must learn to

- create and use representations to organize, record, and communicate mathematical ideas (see Figure 8.1);
- select, apply, and translate among mathematical representations to solve problems; and

- use representations to model and interpret physical, social, and mathematical phenomena.

To provide high-quality math instruction that will meet the Common Core standards and also address the standards of the National Council of Teachers of Mathematics, school administrators can choose from a wide range of mathematics instructional programs for their early childhood classes—Singapore Math, TERC, and Everyday Math, to name a few. The question is, how does an exploratory play-based math center fit in? Any math program opens up opportunities for both teacher and students to innovate and explore, particularly later in the year when children have had lots of experience both with their math curriculum and with center time exploration in the math center. The math center is the perfect place for these innovations and explorations.

Figure 8.1. Zeke put shapes together to look like a boat. He wrote, "I took a shape that looked like a triangle."

Whatever math program you are using with your class can be supplemented and extended at the math center. For example, some New York City schools are using the Go Math! program. If the focus has been on finding multiple ways to show a number, this might become an exploration at the math center. You can challenge children to make up their own number game. You could add blank cards, paper and pencils, spinners, dice, number charts, number lines, and a variety of materials to support this number investigation. To extend the learning even more, invite children to share the games or activities they invented in the math center at the class meeting that ends choice time.

A vibrant, active math center does more than just support the adopted program. Mathematical play empowers children to make decisions about how they use materials, and this helps them develop a sense of agency and self-confidence regarding mathematics. Having mathematical self-confidence and understanding basic concepts related to shape, pattern, and number are

Figure 8.2. Hopscotch in the math center

important as children move toward more abstract math work. Playing with Unifix cubes helps the children in the opening vignette understand and feel confident about concepts that will support them later in the year as they undertake more abstract calculations.

Freely exploring math materials also helps students discover mathematical reasoning. For example, a child might wonder what will happen if she fits triangles together. Discovering she can make a square, she might generalize the idea that four congruent triangles form a square. You could then nudge her further by giving her paper and crayons to record her discovery. Within this simple, playful exploration, the child has incorporated some important steps in mathematical reasoning—investigating, speculating (making a conjecture), generalizing a concept, and representing a finding.

Setting Up the Math Center

Opportunities for mathematical explorations are implicit in many centers—for example, when children measure ingredients to make play dough or look for smaller unit blocks that will equal a larger one. Playing with sand and water supports their understanding of the conservation of numbers. However, the math center gives children opportunities to focus specifically on materials that support mathematical concepts.

In terms of space and location, a math center can go almost anywhere in the classroom. All you need is a space with a table where four, five, or six children can work together. You will also need a place to store math manipulatives, preferably on nearby shelves, but as long as the materials are stored securely, children can take them almost anywhere in the room.

Materials

When it comes to materials in the math center, remember the motto of the minimalist architect Mies van der Rohe: Less is more. Facing an abundance of materials—especially at the start of the school year—may overwhelm children and prevent them from making thoughtful selections.

You can supply the center with a combination of commercial and noncommercial materials, and it's important to rotate them throughout the year to keep student interest fresh. At the beginning of the year, focus on materials that encourage free explorations. Later in the year, the materials will often be connected to your math instruction and you might also have your students help decide which materials to explore in the center.

Here are some commercial materials you might introduce at the beginning of the year. Although most first and second graders will already be familiar with these manipulatives, they still need time for free explorations at the start of the school year.

- Cuisenaire rods
- attribute blocks (These are especially interesting because they have four different attributes—shape, size, depth, and color—see Figures 8.3 and 8.4.)
- geoboards and geobands
- pattern blocks
- Unifix cubes
- pegboards and pegs
- an abacus
- paper and pencils (for recording information).

Figure 8.3. Second graders use attribute blocks to design a house as part of an architecture study.

New materials pique interest, rejuvenate the center, and generate new understanding and explorations. As you think about adding new materials, it's important to have a clear idea of the mathematical concepts you want children to understand. *About Teaching Mathematics*, by Marilyn Burns (2007), provides valuable background information that will help you decide what new materials to introduce, when to intervene with observations and suggestions, and what types of suggestions and challenges are appropriate.

Figure 8.4. Measuring attribute blocks

After children have explored basic math materials, you might add some of the following supplemental materials to deepen their explorations when it seems children are ready.

- dice
- tangrams
- games from your math program
- grid paper and colored pencils (to plan designs for geoboards)
- graph paper and colored pencils
- board games
- dominoes
- decks of playing cards
- spinners and counters
- rulers and tape measures (helpful for making blueprints and plans)
- magnifying glasses (for exploring minting dates on coins)
- a variety of scales (balance scale, kitchen scale, bathroom scale)
- clocks (digital and analog)
- tessellation packs or puzzles
- origami paper
- checker sets and, if children seem ready for it, chess sets
- unbreakable mirrors (large enough to place under pattern blocks—great for seeing patterns and designs in new ways).

There are also many effective noncommercial materials that can support all sorts of mathematical explorations. Basically anything that can be counted, sorted, or measured is fair game. Here are a few possibilities:

- keys (real estate offices and locksmiths often have lots of keys to give away)
- buttons (all sizes, shapes, and colors—see Figure 8.5)
- acorns
- fabric squares (from fabric sample catalogs)
- bottle caps and corks
- seashells
- pennies

- old game boards (re-covered with white paper)
- toothpicks, paper clips, Popsicle sticks (for nontraditional measuring, among other uses).

Organization and Guidelines

All the materials for the math center and the shelves where they're stored should be labeled in some way so that children know where to find things and where to return them when they are finished. In kindergarten, you might put a picture on the appropriate shelf area. Then, as the children begin to write words at the end of kindergarten or the start of first grade, introduce a label-the-room

Figure 8.5. Children sort buttons in the mathematics center.

activity and have them add word labels to the picture ones. As their spelling becomes more accurate, replace the invented-spelling labels with new labels on which the words are conventionally spelled. The children will gain a greater sense of ownership and have a practical use for their writing skills.

Typically, children don't need a lot of rules or guidelines to use and care for the math center. If the materials are appropriate and have been introduced at a class meeting, children should be able to use the center independently from the beginning of the school year. However, certain manipulatives may invite chaotic play. Some children, for example, won't be able to help themselves from swinging colored chain links around or dragging them about. If you suspect certain materials might inspire chaotic play, establish clear guidelines for their use with children, or simply don't use them for free, self-directed explorations.

Launching the Math Center

Regardless of the age of the children you teach, it's best to start the year with a period of free exploration in the math center. While each grade level benefits from free explorations, there are increasing levels of sophistication across the grades. In prekindergarten and kindergarten, many of the materials such as attribute blocks, pattern blocks, and geoboards are new and exciting because they are completely unfamiliar. First and second graders will review ways of

Figure 8.6. Building structures with clay and toothpicks in the mathematics center

using the materials introduced in kindergarten and explore new materials—a sand clock and a kitchen timer, straws and connectors (small pieces of play dough work well; see Figure 8.6), a set of pentominoes. Having time to acquaint and reacquaint themselves with various math materials and explore them freely prepares children for more sophisticated explorations later.

As you launch the center at the beginning of the school year, begin simply and introduce different math materials one at a time in a class meeting. After you have briefly modeled ways of using a particular manipulative, give children an opportunity to try it out as a whole class. After a few minutes of exploration, discuss children's observations and note them on a chart. It's important to be open to all ideas children have for using the materials. After the meeting, add the new manipulative to the math center and let children experiment on their own. By observing and listening to their play and early explorations, you'll gather information about children's mathematical understanding and how they interact and share information.

Pattern blocks are a great first manipulative for launching the math center; they are appealing and accessible, and children can use them in a variety of ways without much support. In *Mathematics: The Science of Patterns*, Keith Devlin defines mathematics as "the study of patterns—real or imagined, visual or mental, arising from the natural world or from within the human mind" (1997, 6). Much of children's work at the math center naturally gravitates toward an exploration of patterns, so this is another reason that pattern blocks are a good first exploration.

By observing children as they work with pattern blocks, you can get a quick snapshot of children's prior knowledge, skills, and interests: *Joseph is sorting the shapes by color. Marigold arranges the shapes in patterns. Joshua seems to know a lot about space and rocket ships; he's using all the available shapes to create a detailed spaceship!* By observing and questioning, you will learn so much about children's understanding of shape and pattern:

- How do they use the blocks?
- Do they begin by sorting them?
- Do they stack one on top of the other?
- Who is creating pictures with the shapes?
- Are children talking to one another about their patterns, or are they working solitarily without any peer interactions?
- Are they referring to the names of the shapes?

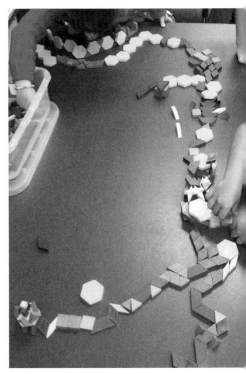

Figure 8.7. Constructing a pattern-block playground

Making observations and posing questions also lets you know when to add new materials and challenges. Watching his students use pattern blocks, Bill Fulbrecht realized that they were ready to extend their explorations. The class was studying playgrounds, and Bill challenged the children to build a pattern-block playground. The children excitedly collaborated on constructing their version of a playground, using what they knew about playgrounds and what they had learned about the different shapes that they worked with (see Figure 8.7).

Connecting the Math Center to Instruction

At the beginning of the year, children do a lot of playful experimenting with the materials in the math center, but later in kindergarten and first grade, they begin to make connections to the mathematics being learned in class. For example, at the beginning of kindergarten, children might explore Cuisenaire rods without considering much math (*I'm going to make a purple snake*), but later they might use these same materials in more sophisticated ways (*I made a snake with ten orange rods. Let's see which snake has more rods*).

Over time, children will have many opportunities to freely explore mathematical materials during center time and find their own unique ways of using them. As the year progresses, however, materials and games in the math center should prompt children to explore what they are learning in their mathematics lessons. As children are developing new mathematical understandings and strategies for solving problems, they enjoy practicing many of the games and activities that were introduced in their lessons. For example, children might begin by playing a game you've introduced during math time, and as you observe, you might decide to introduce a new material or suggest a new game that builds on their work. You can also connect math center activities to other studies. First graders studying money could explore various coins and learn new coin games. They might look closely at the details on the coins through a magnifying class, sort the coins based on these details, and graph the results. You could be encouraging future coin collectors—numismatists!

Many mathematics programs model using calculators for quick computation. Children at the math center might use their new calculator and computation skills to play a game like beat the calculator, where two children turn over cards with mathematical problems and compete against each other to see who can come up with the answer first: the child who uses the calculator or the child who solves the problem mentally.

As children learn the concepts of *more than* and *less than* and develop a sense of the progression of numbers, they might use these newly learned skills to play a number squeeze game. The Everyday Math program calls this game the Monster Squeeze. One child thinks of a number. Using a number line or a number chart, the other children try to guess the number by asking questions such as, "Is it more than ten?" and "Is it less than fifty?" They eventually squeeze out the other numbers until they get really close to the secret number. The more times children play this game, the more adept they get at asking the best *more* or *less* questions! The math center, filled with opportunities to support your math curriculum, opens up many ways of using a variety of materials to explore math concepts across the school year.

Spotlight on Inquiry-Driven Centers

Katie Rust and Andrew Mastin's first-grade class, along with all of the other first grades in their school, were studying markets. The teachers and children went on many trips to local markets, interviewed the workers, and wrote about their observations and experiences. Then something happened that shook up their study.

The turning point happened on a trip to a large farmers' market in Manhattan. The children had never seen anything like the market and they were stunned. Where were the cash registers? There weren't any aisles! Where was the conveyor belt?

Picking up on the children's questions, the teachers approached one of the vegetable stands and invited the farmer to speak with the children. He explained how the produce was grown on his farm and how he and his farmhands harvested the crops. His explanation introduced new vocabulary and concepts and provoked even more questions from the group of six-year-olds. None of the children had ever been to a working farm, although some had visited the farm animal exhibit at a zoo.

Upon returning to the classroom, the children were excited and eager to learn more about farms and produce, so Katie and Andrew arranged a trip to a farm and also to a local vegetable garden. Out of these experiences, many new center explorations evolved, most of them suggested by the children. They created a planting center, a worm and compost center, and a center where they used market sales flyers to compare prices and determine the most economical place to shop for food in their neighborhood. In the dramatic play center, children used storyboards to plan a market drama and act it out. At the block center, the children used the whiteboard to make a plan for a market and then they spent the week building and labeling it, including a loading dock too. At the sewing center, children designed and made clothes for a life-size model of a farmer. (See Figures 8.8, 8.9, and 8.10.)

Figure 8.8. Gathering soil

Figure 8.9. Learning to use a sewing machine to sew clothes for the farmer

Figure 8.10. Making a life-size model of a farmer

When I visited the class, the children were eager to share their center activities with me. They were particularly proud of the life-size, fully dressed model of a farmer that stood front and center in their classroom!

Enhancing and Enriching the Math Center

Later in the year, the math center is an exciting place where all sorts of interesting innovations based on mathematical connections are happening. The possibilities for enhancing and enriching the center are almost endless, so you'll need to think about the children you teach and their interests as well as the curriculum at your particular grade level to decide on the enrichments that make the most sense for your center. What follows are some of my most successful ideas for enhancing the work of the center.

Create Board Games

When children play board and card games, they draw on their understandings of number sequence, concepts of *before* and *after*, and understanding of *greater than* and *less than*. They also learn the importance of careful strategizing. In the math center, children have had many opportunities to learn the strategies and rules necessary to play a variety of board games (Candy Land, checkers, and chess); card games (go fish, concentration, and crazy eights); calculator games (beat the calculator); and guessing games (guess my rule). Now you might encourage children to innovate on some familiar games.

To support children in creating their own board and card games, you can first brainstorm ideas for games based on favorite read-aloud books or concepts related to a class study. For example, children in one first-grade math center created a board game based on *Mr. Popper's Penguins*, a book their teacher had read aloud. Once children have chosen a theme for their game, supply them with blank game boards, blank cards, writing implements (markers, pencils, colored pencils), dice, blank spinners, and chips. Encourage children to pay attention to how game rules are formatted and then compose rules for their game. Perhaps create a checklist of the attributes of game instruction. Have the game's creators share their game with the class, answering any questions, and add the new game to the math center. Encourage children who are having difficulty understanding the rules to have the "experts" who created the game help them learn to play it.

Write Math Stories and Puzzles

In his memoir, *The Sky Is Not the Limit*, Neil deGrasse Tyson (2004) shares a story about a friend teaching him the "game" of writing brain teasers—clever, short mathematical stories with interesting twists. This could be a challenging math center innovation for second graders who might be ready for using their math and writing skills to create math puzzles. You might even compile the puzzles children create into a math word puzzle book!

Conduct a Survey

The process of designing and carrying out a survey places children within a complex and sophisticated situation. They must collaborate in constructing important, well-worded questions. They discover the necessity of carefully recording data. They have the opportunity for authentic practice in tallying and using tallies to count and record numbers. If they take the next step and use their information to create graphs, these authentic graphing experiences help them appreciate the importance of interpreting the information found on their graphs.

Figure 8.11. A kindergartner designed a survey to collect data about classmates' favorite colors.

One way to begin is to review the survey process as a class. Discuss the attributes of a good survey question. If children suggest, "Which is your favorite flavor of ice cream: vanilla, strawberry, or chocolate?" you might say, "But my favorite is pistachio. I wonder if anyone else has a different favorite flavor?" Eventually children will understand that there needs to be an opt-out category—"none of these"—or that the question needs to be reworded. Then tally some responses, add them up, and decide how to represent the information. Create a graph together, and invite children to interpret the information on the graph.

After a whole-class experience, challenge the children at the math center to create their own survey questions (see Figure 8.11), gather and tally data (see Figure 8.12), and represent this information on a graph (will they use pictures, names, or colors?). Also encourage them to find a way to share their information. They can write a narrative, lead a group discussion at the class meeting, or perhaps think of some other means.

Figure 8.12. Taking a survey

Display the graph and any writing done in connection with it in the math center. (This will take several choice time sessions.)

Measure: How Big Is My Foot?

Young children, particularly children in prekindergarten and kindergarten (and even some first graders), are still figuring out size relationships. It's not unusual to hear a kindergarten child refer to an object as being "as big as." *My daddy is so big, like a giant!* This activity gives children opportunities to use a variety of materials to express the length of their feet. Children begin by tracing one of their feet on oak tag and then cutting out the tracing. Then they can measure their foot using whatever nonstandard materials they choose—paper clips, pencils, Unifix cubes, beads, and so on—first recording a guess and then, next to it, the actual measurement. Their predictions will become more accurate with experience.

The more nonstandard materials children use, the greater their understanding of size relationships. Children begin to realize that it will take fewer drinking straws to go across their foot cutout than buttons, or that they will need more paper clips to measure their foot than pipe cleaners. They gain a greater understanding of the relationship between lengths and objects.

Create with Origami

Even on the simplest level, when children engage in origami projects, they are having experiences with recognizing shapes and patterns. As they fold and unfold the origami paper, a complex pattern of geometric designs reveals itself (see www.paperfolding.com). Children can look for different shapes. How many triangles can they find? Any squares? What did they do to make these shapes? Older children might be introduced to origami puzzles, through which they can discover shape and color patterns.

The translation of the Japanese word *origami* is "folding paper." Children manipulate a square of origami paper into different shapes—a sailboat, a bird, or an insect, for example—to create a paper sculpture. There are many books of easy origami patterns for children to follow, and patterns can also be downloaded from the Internet. In the process, children learn about fractions (as they fold the paper) and increase their mathematical vocabulary (*diagonal, symmetry*, *intersecting planes*). They often need help with some of the directions for creating the objects; this encourages them to help one another and sometimes assume the role of teacher. When they master the art of origami, they feel a tremendous sense of empowerment!

Make Play Dough

The process of making play dough actually incorporates lots of different skills, but math is prominently on display as children measure the ingredients. Every Monday in my classroom, I had a group of children make a new batch of play dough for the week. I used a recipe for uncooked play dough because I wanted the children to have the experience of immersing their hands in the dough throughout the entire procedure. A recipe chart, illustrated with simple pictures and only a few words, blocked out the steps in the process (see Figure 8.13 for another teacher's example).

Figure 8.13. Connie's play dough recipe chart

The play dough center should evolve over the year. At first children will be interested in the different textures of the ingredients and observing the changes that happen to the dry ingredients when water is added. You might begin making play dough using water without coloring, but later, children can add food coloring, a different color each week. Children might experiment by adding spices for aromatic play dough, sand for gritty play dough, and glitter for sparkly play dough. By the last few months of the year, children should be able to make their own play dough, using recipe books they've written and small bowls, cups, and spoons. If you give them zip-top bags, they can label the bags with their names and take the play dough home along with their recipe books.

Use Literacy Skills

Children need a variety of literacy skills to convey what they know and can do in mathematics. Opportunities for enriching the math center with literacy include the following:

- using a variety of graphic organizers to organize and explain mathematical findings
- learning and understanding how to use new vocabulary
- following directions
- reading texts connected to mathematical explorations (e.g., Arnold Lobel's story "The Lost Button" from *Frog and Toad* with a guess-the-rule activity; *How Big Is a Foot?* by Rolf Myller, with a measuring activity; *The Great Pet Sale*, by Mike Inkpen, when working with coins; Molly Bang's *The Paper Crane* when creating origami; Jannelle Martin's *ABC Math Riddles* when creating riddles)
- recording math discoveries in a math journal.

Teaching Interventions in the Math Center

You can support children's mathematical understanding by observing how they use math materials at the center and intervening with challenges and questions. See the chart for some examples of typical kinds of observations and possible teaching interventions.

Teaching Interventions

Observation	Possible Response
Toby and James are each making designs with pattern blocks. They are working side by side but not interacting with each other.	"Toby, I wonder if you could use the geoboard to copy the design James is making? Then perhaps you could switch places and James could copy Toby's pattern. Let me know how that works out."
Linda and Kayla are playing tic-tac-toe. They seem to be adding Xs and Os haphazardly and you think they are ready to be more strategic about their moves.	"Linda and Kayla, I'd like to come back in a few minutes to watch you play this interesting game. Perhaps when I come back you can share with me some of your thinking about why you put the Xs and Os in different squares. I can't wait to find out what your strategies were!"
The children at the center seem to be using materials without careful selection or purpose. You wonder if the center is becoming stale.	"What might we add to the math center to make it more challenging?" (Ask either the children at the center or the whole class.)
Malik and Nelson are using the Cuisenaire rods to make designs. You have been discussing symmetry during math lessons and would like them to make connections.	"Malik and Nelson, would you like to use these small mirrors to find symmetrical copies of these patterns?"
Children are figuring out ways of making ten with cubes. You want to deepen their conceptual thinking by challenging them to articulate their decisions.	"Can you describe three different ways for showing the number ten? Is there a way you can record this?"

Observation	Possible Response
A group of second graders working with a pile of pennies seems to be unfocused, mainly moving the pennies about between each other.	"I wonder if you could use these magnifying glasses to find information you can use to organize your pennies in new ways?"
First graders are working with geoboards and geobands, making designs and talking about the fractions they are creating. You have been studying halves in math class and would like to challenge them to think out of the box and discover more complex halves.	"Do you think you could use crooked lines to divide the geoboards into halves? When you figure out how to do this, record what you did on graph paper. You can share your findings with the class, and we'll leave your recordings at the center."

Thoughtful observations and challenging questions raise children's playful explorations of math materials to higher levels of inquiry and understanding. Connections you make between your whole-class instruction, children's independent explorations, and the support you give their mathematical investigations will ensure that they are engaged in purposeful mathematical learning.

> It took me four years to paint like Raphael, but a lifetime to paint like a child.
>
> —Pablo Picasso

Art Center

Howard Ikemoto, an artist *who taught studio classes for thirty-four years at Cabrillo College, in California, remembers this exchange with his daughter: "When my daughter was about seven years old, she asked me one day what I did at work. I told her I worked at the college—that my job was to teach people how to draw. She stared at me, incredulous, and said, 'You mean they forget?'" (Butler 2016)*

As Ikemoto's child so innocently reminded her father, children are natural artists. My artist husband, Simon Dinnerstein, defines art as "an intensely personal, charged, poetic, and transcendent response to life." The art center is where children can express their responses to life in myriad ways. A four-year-old's crayon swirl represents a story about a trip to the beach. A bright orange sun painted across an open sky communicates joy and energy. A small house constructed of colored paper says *home*.

When we adopt an expansive definition of literacy (beyond reading and writing) that includes self-expression through art, we open up new avenues into the literate world for the children we teach. Neither Michelangelo nor Picasso was interested in school or academics, but Michelangelo was obsessed with drawing and sculpting, and Picasso was so artistically talented that he was admitted to Barcelona's prestigious School of Fine Arts at the age of fourteen. This is not to say that we shouldn't teach all children reading and writing. However, it's incredibly important to value children's individual and unique artistic personalities in our classrooms. For some children, recognition of and pride in their artistic experiences can give them the confidence they need to tackle more challenging areas of the curriculum.

The art center, or studio, gives children risk-free opportunities to explore a variety of art materials and experiment with many techniques. Children should see the art center as a place of experimentation where they don't necessarily need to create a product to hang on the wall. Andy Warhol, an artist who broke many of the traditional rules of fine art, said, "An artist is somebody who produces things that people don't need to have" (Randolph 2011).

As they explore as artists, children develop many important habits of mind. In *The Artistic Edge: Seven Skills Children Need to Succeed in an Increasingly Right Brain World*, Lisa Phillips (2012) discusses ten different cognitive skills and art program supports: creativity, confidence, problem solving, perseverance, nonverbal communication, focus, ability to receive constructive feedback, collaboration, dedication, and accountability. Although these skills are supported in all centers, they are particularly important in the art center, where children's budding self-esteem is tied closely to their pride in their artistic achievements.

The art center is also where children have opportunities to practice many new technical art skills: using scissors, refining gluing techniques, learning different ways of folding, rolling, and crinkling paper, and many more. Children control how and what they create using the materials you provide. As

Figure 9.1. Using tools in the art center to create a paper purse

they cut, paint, draw, and sculpt, you scaffold their growing confidence and independence with your support and encouragement.

New York City's Department of Education, acknowledging the importance of various art forms in a child's education, has created a blueprint for the arts, a plan that recognizes the value of visual literacy and sets benchmarks for various strands of visual learning. Describing early childhood and grade 2 benchmarks, Professor Judith Burton's introduction says:

Young children are active and exuberant explorers. Artistic images capture the physical and sensory aspects of their discoveries. . . . Art making becomes an important spur to the use of imagination. (Burton 2015, 4)

Setting Up the Art Center or Studio

Roger Thérond (2001) describes the studio of the Spanish artist Joan Miró as "meticulously organized." He explains, "The brushes are aligned for his personal ritual. He paints according to how he feels. . . . Miro has the freedom to create what he wants, when he wants" (104). Miro's art studio brings to mind Joseph Campbell's description of "the place of creative incubation [where] you can simply experience and bring forth what you are and what you might be" (1988, 92).

An art studio in a classroom has to support the "personal rituals" of a whole group of young children, of course, so thinking carefully about how the center will best support the children you teach is important.

Space and Location

The art center is not a particularly noisy or active center, so you don't have to worry about its location in that regard, but you will need some space. Two-sided easels for painting are considered standard equipment in an art center, and it's best if you can have at least two of them. The first question you'll need to ask is "Where do I have room for stand-alone easels?" If floor space is limited, you can mount easels on the wall, or you can cover part of a wall with heavy plastic and affix paper to it (this works especially well for murals).

Children working on art projects need large spaces on which to lay out materials. Two connected tables should provide enough workspace. Cover tables with plastic shower curtains to keep them from getting stained with crayon, glue, and paint. You might consider placing plastic on the floor underneath the easels as well.

If you don't have room for a dedicated space for the art center, there are other options. Studio in a School, an organization that sends professional artists into New York City schools, works with children and teachers to develop quality art experiences. The artists help teachers create art studios using a simple, easy-to-follow template. The Studio in a School prototype needs only a small bookcase to hold materials (see Figures 9.2 and 9.3).

The bottom shelf holds a variety of collage materials—pieces of fabric, buttons, sequins, recycled materials, strips of different-colored and different-textured paper. On the second shelf there are trays and baskets of watercolor paints, cups, brushes, and sponges. There's also a bucket of wood pieces. The top shelf holds markers, crayons, pencils, chalk, glue, and scissors, and large sheets of paper are kept on top of the bookcase.

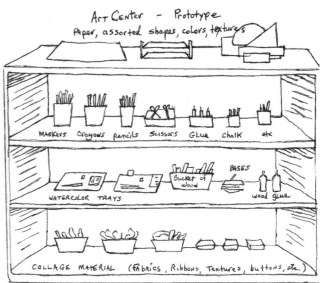

Figure 9.2. Art shelf template inspired by Studio in a School

Figure 9.3. An artists' corner

An airtight container for clay is on the floor next to the bookcase, and there are clay boards (the backs of old wooden puzzles are great substitutes) and a plastic tablecloth in an adjoining basket.

Displays

Thinking carefully about the arrangement and ambiance of the classroom is the first step in supporting children's early artwork. You could display images of early American quilts and weavings, Native American art, African sculptures, Jackson Pollack drip paintings, Calder mobiles, or Monet and van Gogh floral paintings. In the art center itself, children should be inspired by images of all varieties of art. A basket of art postcards and other types of reproductions makes a perfect display. These images are an early introduction to art history, exposing children to the wide range of possibilities artists have explored through the ages and inviting them to become members of the artistic community.

You might also consider displaying baskets of books about art and artists to encourage children to appreciate techniques used by professionals. You can often find coffee-table books filled with paintings by famous artists at thrift stores or yard sales. Children also enjoy reading stories about artists, so consider adding some of these recommended titles:

- *Little Blue and Little Yellow*, *A Color of His Own*, and *Matthew's Dream*, all by Leo Lionni
- *Harold and the Purple Crayon*, by Crockett Johnson
- *Mouse Paint*, by Ellen Stoll Walsh
- *The Fantastic Jungles of Henri Rousseau*, by Michelle Markel
- *Vincent's Colors*, by Victoria Charles

Children can also use a basket of how-to books in the art center to help them learn specific techniques. Here are some suggested titles:

- *Ed Emberley's Drawing Book of Animals*, by Ed Emberley
- *Cartooning for Kids*, by Mike Artell
- *Color and Collage Origami Art*, by Andrew Dewar
- *Calligraphy for Kids*, by Eleanor Winters
- *Kids' Paper Airplane Book*, by Ken Blackburn
- *Clay Play!* by Terry Taylor
- *3-D Art Lab for Kids*, by Susan Schwake

Materials

Even if you have a large area set aside for the art studio, it's best to keep the simplicity of the Studio in a School shelf in mind. It's important to provide a limited selection of clear, attractive, and interesting materials and to rotate them regularly. Unlike most other centers, the materials in the art center will need ongoing care and replenishment, so you'll need a plan for restocking. You might invite your students to help you make a schedule for caring for the disposable materials.

While many materials will rotate in and out of the art center, some will need to be housed there permanently, including these:

- sharpened pencils
- crayons (It pays to get good-quality ones; the colors they produce are more vibrant and denser.)
- scissors (Create a scissors holder by poking holes in a Styrofoam cube or a large upturned can.)
- glue
- adhesive tape
- watercolor paints (I have prekindergartners and kindergartners use crayons rather than paint the first week of school until I've demonstrated how to use and wash the brushes.)
- brushes of different thicknesses so children can experiment with a variety of painted lines
- smocks

- construction paper of different sizes and colors
- large sheets of newsprint
- white and manila drawing paper

Figure 9.4. Working with twigs in the art center

New materials can stimulate new excitement about and interest in the art center. Odilon Redon, the French painter of mysterious symbolist images, wrote, "The artist yields often to the stimuli of materials that will transmit his spirit" (Ernst 2014). Introducing interesting or beautiful materials, particularly things found in nature, like rose petals, twigs, and beautiful pebbles (see Figure 9.4), might inspire new, unexpected creations. Be ready to add or rotate more sophisticated materials as children are ready for them. Here are a few possibilities:

- *Drawing implements:* Provide colored pencils, chalk, calligraphy ink pens, and Cray-Pas oil pastels.
- *Finger paints:* For young children, particularly in prekindergarten and kindergarten, finger painting is a sensual experience. Because they use their hands and fingers, they are also strengthening their fine motor skills. Since finger-paint paper can be expensive, you might have children paint directly on the table using washable finger paint and then use any type of paper to capture the images. It's messy but a wonderful way for children to dig right in and freely express themselves. If they don't like what they have drawn, they can wipe it off and start over!
- *Tempera paints:* Limiting choices to white, black, and the primary colors lets children discover how mixing primary colors creates new colors. Most easels have a lower shelf where you can store these paints.

- *Wet-on-wet painting:* Watercolor painting on paper made wet with a sponge creates an image in which the colors melt into one another.
- *Crayon resist painting:* Watercolor painting over a drawing made with a white wax crayon makes the crayon image seem to appear magically.
- *Mural paper:* Mural paper is particularly good for group painting projects that support a class study (a frieze of the neighborhood, for example).
- *Wood scraps and commercial wooden objects:* Use these for three-dimensional constructions and assemblages.
- *Staplers.*

Guidelines

Respect is the most important guideline—everyone needs to recognize the seriousness of the work being done and treat the artists and art in an appropriate way. Some children are able to draw extremely sophisticated figurative drawings. Other children enjoy experimenting with color and shape. Appreciation and respect for all artists and art forms are important attitudes for children to learn and should be the subject of ongoing class discussions. *Matthew's Dream*, by Leo Lionni, is an ideal book to read aloud before initiating a discussion about appreciating new art forms and discovering oneself through art.

Respect for the art materials and organization is also essential. Children need to learn that they should not waste paper, they should cover markers when they are done with them, they must wash paintbrushes and return them to the paintbrush container, and they need to cover paint pots. Related to this, children need to respect the center's organization and understand the importance of returning materials to their correct place on shelves so that other children can find the items they need (Figure 9.5). And finally, safety is

Figure 9.5. Clear bins help children independently organize the art center.

Figure 9.6. Focused attentively on using watercolor paints

important when children are using scissors or staplers; the use of such tools must be explicitly taught and practiced. Children need to learn to hold the sharp ends of scissors in their fists when they aren't using them so they won't accidentally stab anyone.

Launching the Art Center

When you launch the art center, it helps to start with an appealing provocation. I often use large sunflowers (in a vase or just laid out on a table) or beautiful seashells and other beach artifacts. Accompany this display with a basket containing reproductions of related artworks by various artists, some representative (realistic), some abstract. The beauty of the display and the variety of art reproductions will entice children to create their own crayon drawings. Francesca, a former kindergarten student of mine who is now a college graduate, remembers her first day of kindergarten: "I was worried. I had never been away from my parents for a long time before. But I sat down at a table you'd set up and started to copy a sunflower and decided I was fine with kindergarten. So I got up, kissed my parents good-bye, and they left."

You will need to launch any new material you add to the center by introducing it at a class meeting. Demonstrate techniques for using the new material rather than a completed product. Let children figure out on their own how they might use that technique in their work. Then give the whole class time to work with the new material and share what they have created.

For example, if you're adding markers, show children how to cap them and have them listen

Figure 9.7. Trying new materials

for the click when the cap is secure. Then give each child a marker and have a practice capping session. When you add glue to the center, first demonstrate how to use a small amount of glue when pasting pieces of paper or fabric onto a collage. Have the whole class help you make a collage so that the students have a guided experience using the glue. When introducing paper sculpting using strips of paper, show children various techniques for shaping a paper strip—folding it like a fan or twirling it around a crayon to make a curl. Encourage children to give it a try and to invent their own way to fold or twirl a paper strip. Then show them how to paste it to the backing paper or to another strip, holding it down for a count of twenty so that it will adhere (creating paper sculptures that don't hold together can be very frustrating).

Spotlight on Inquiry-Driven Centers

At the art center, a group of children in Dana Roth's kindergarten class became fascinated by the variety of colors they could mix. Dana first put out red, yellow, blue, white, and black paint. After the children discovered they could mix the paint to create purple, green, pink, and orange, Dana challenged them to see if they could make different shades of these colors. The children became more and more excited by the different shades they were creating. Children from other centers began stopping by to see what all the excitement was about. The popularity of the center grew.

Next, Dana challenged the children to see if they could figure out how many daubs of paint it took to make each color. She suggested they might want to create a chart to show how they made a new color. How much red did they mix with the yellow to create the dark, dark orange? Which colors and how much of each did they use to make the light, airy green? The children drew on both math and literacy skills to create the chart.

After the children worked on the new challenge for a few days, Dana brought in a very large box of crayons. She scattered all the crayons on the art table and the children scrambled to try out the many colors. Dana suggested the children look at the names of the colors, and she began reading different ones: *Flaming red. Violet. Pumpkin orange.* The children

Figure 9.8. Experimenting with color

gave Dana more and more colors so they could hear all of the different names. Dana wondered aloud, "Hmm, I wonder what kinds of unusual and interesting names you might give the colors on your chart?" This was all it took to set the children off on a color-naming frenzy! Soon all of the colors on their chart were blessed with interesting (and often silly) names. After the children shared the chart with the class, Dana assured them the center would remain open as long as there was an interest.

Enhancing and Enriching the Art Center

Introduce New Forms of Art

Any time you add new materials to the center, you set the stage for children to discover many new rich possibilities as artists. But in addition to materials, it's important to introduce children to new kinds of art as well. Collage, for example, is a specific kind of art children may not have experienced and wouldn't think to make on their own. Sample wallpaper books are great raw material for collage. Decorator stores are good sources; owners or managers usually have books of discontinued samples they will give you for free. Weaving is another art form that offers many possibilities for creativity. Begin by having children weave with different kinds of paper and follow up by introducing other forms of weaving. Demonstrate finger weaving and weaving with sticks and embroidery hoops (you can use Hula-Hoops for group projects). Sewing is another engaging art form (see Figure 9.9).

Connect Art to Class Studies

During the school year, projects in the art center can be connected to class studies. A class studying the concept and physical makeup of a neighborhood, for example, might create a neighborhood mural.

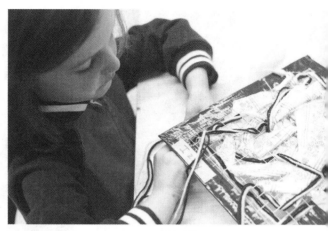

Figure 9.9. Izzy creates a multimedia collage with yarn, fabric, and mesh.

One of my art center groups constructed a model of a human skeleton when the class was studying human and animal skeletons. They made the head of papier-mâché and created the body parts using an egg carton for vertebrae, Plasticine for discs, and paper dowels and Popsicle sticks for other bones. After it was completed, they labeled the parts (see Figure 9.10).

Similarly, first graders studying turtles (their pet turtle, Shelly, in particular) used the materials in the art center to create turtle images in different ways: some used clay, some made drawings, and others painted (see Figures 9.11 and 9.12).

Incorporate Literacy

Making astute and sensitive observations in the art studio helps children develop visual literacy—the ability to "read" images and symbols, to use an image to communicate meaning (Edwards 2010). Developing this literacy is an important enrichment. Over time,

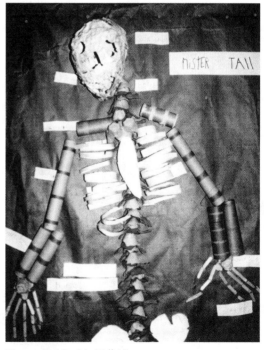

Figure 9.10. Mr. Tall Man

Figure 9.11. Sculpting turtles

Figure 9.12. Shelley paints a turtle.

Figure 9.13. Page from the artist Simon Dinnerstein's sketchbook

children should become familiar with terms such as *shape*, *line*, *texture*, and *pattern*. This increased vocabulary plays a significant role in scaffolding children's intellectual and cognitive development (Tough 1976).

When children follow directions for making things like origami or calligraphy, their reading skills are supported. Using books to research new projects and explore the work of established artists also supports children as readers. Books such as Tomie dePaola's *The Art Lesson* and Leo Lionni's *Matthew's Dream* have art as their theme and are wonderful enrichments for the center. And children can write about art as well, of course. Consider supplying the center with "sketchbooks" (a few sheets of paper stapled together) and showing children examples of how artists not only draw sketches but also write down important words and observations that they then use to inspire new projects (see Figure 9.13).

Teaching Interventions in the Art Center

The way you respond to children's artwork is the key to supporting their early and more advanced work. You want them to be independent and confident, just as they are in writing workshop; you don't want them to be dependent on your approval.

The chart that follows provides some suggestions for teaching interventions you might make in common situations.

Teaching Interventions

Observation	Possible Response
A child asks you what you think of his drawing, painting, or other artistic creation.	Say, "I'm so curious to know what you were thinking about when you made this interesting picture." This should initiate a conversation about the work rather than encourage reliance on your approval.
A child complains that she doesn't know what to do next.	Instead of telling her what to do, ask, "What do *you* think would work next?"
A child has made a particularly beautiful piece of art.	Stay away from responses such as *good job*, *beautiful*, or other words of approval. Instead, be more specific. "That orange line really interests me. Tell me about it." Or point out something you notice. "I notice you use lots of bright colors."

continues

Observation	Possible Response
Children are mixing colors in interesting ways at the easel.	Recognize and support the experimentation and discoveries children are making. "What an interesting way to mix colors together. I wonder if you will find other colors when you mix your paints."
A child has made a piece of art that just doesn't appeal to you aesthetically.	Never judge a piece of artwork negatively. All artists, children included, are exposing a deeply sensitive part of themselves when they share their artwork. Negative criticism can have lasting repercussions.

The art studio is a place where children create personal works of art inspired by their imagination and use the visual arts to extend a class investigation. It is a pathway for visually expressing feelings and ideas they might not be able to communicate in other ways. It is here they learn, as the French artist Edgar Degas wrote, that "art is not what you see, but what you make others see."

> I'm finished with something, but I'm not beginning anything. That's wrong. When you finish something, you ought always to begin something new.
>
> —**Maud Hart Lovelace,** *Emily of Deep Valley*

Moving Forward

Letting Children Take Ownership

Sometime around the end of the fall, centers will be functioning in full swing. You might be sighing with relief as you see that all is working well. Now your emphasis will most likely shift from the challenge of setting up interesting and stimulating centers to keeping these centers lively, engaging, and expanding. You're moving from a focus on developing well-managed centers toward supporting centers that children develop. You are now giving your students greater autonomy as they investigate topics that interest them and find an outlet for their passions.

Children will be using materials with more independence and will understand choice time routines. You will be fascinated to observe children demonstrating their interests and personalities as they opt for the activities that appeal to them. Centers begin to incorporate children's growing interests and ideas. Inquiry, exploration, and discovery become what Tim O'Keefe, a teacher of seven- and eight-year-olds at the Center for Inquiry in South Carolina, describes as "a habit of the heart and mind" (Mills 2015, 40).

Children will begin taking greater initiative in creating new centers and extending the possibilities for how to use materials in existing centers. Children's engagement is particularly noticeable when a class is entrenched in a project that has worked its way into the centers at choice time. A classroom where children are intensely involved in an important study emits a buzz of excitement.

Choice time centers can provide opportunities for children to engage in personal inquiries that inspire them to imagine new possibilities for exploration. When this happens, the classroom becomes a community where children and teachers find each other "successful socially, emotionally, personally and also academically" (Johnston and Ivey 2015, 61).

The delight of tapping into children's curiosity and creativity and walking with them on the path toward lifelong learning makes teaching a prized and honored profession. In *Learning for Real*, Heidi Mills (2014) reminds us how exhilarating it is when we are given the opportunity "to learn something new, to develop expertise around a passion, to share with a community, to learn alongside others who are deeply interested in the same topic, sport or hobby" (xix). Your enthusiasm and desire to include inquiry-based centers will rise to the challenge of making children's playful explorations an exciting experience for your children and for you.

Appendix A
Planning Tool for Centers

Center:
Instructional rationale for setting up this center:
Materials and physical setup of the center: (You might include a sketch of the layout of the center.)
What materials can be added to support inquiry and exploration in this center? (Add this information after observing how children are using the center.)
Are there any connections that can be made between this center and classroom studies and inquiry projects?

Observation and Reflection Form for Centers

Date: Center: Children:		
Observations	**Reflections on Observations**	**Next Steps**

Acknowledgments

When I was a new teacher in the late 1960s, my anxiety about doing a good job and my fear of losing control led me to literally tie desks together in straight rows. I believed that if rows were straight and children were seated quietly at their desks, I was doing a good job. I look back on those years with great embarrassment and wish that I could send a personal apology to the six- and seven-years-olds who bore the first years of my teaching with relatively little complaint! As a Chinese proverb says, "to get through the hardest journey, we need take only one step at a time, but we must keep on stepping." This book represents almost a half-century of taking baby steps. I have many people to thank—former school colleagues, friends and collaborators, and family—for helping me along that path.

My first year, I was terrified that my inexperience would mess up the futures of thirty-four second-grade children. I didn't know where to begin. Jennifer Monaghan, the PTA president, came to the rescue by introducing me to the formidable Oma Riggs. Both of these strong and dedicated women were instrumental in instilling in me the belief that all children could learn to read and write and gave me some tools to make it happen. Although my style of teaching has changed over the years, I'm forever appreciative of the support they gave me and for the belief systems they generously shared with a young, inexperienced teacher.

At PS 321 I benefited from the strong and progressive leadership of William Casey, Peter Heaney, and Liz Phillips. They each gave me opportunities to grow as a teacher and to experiment with new ideas that I brought to my classroom. How fortunate I was to work in a community of caring and intelligent educators. I particularly must shout out thanks to Bill Fulbrecht and Barbara Taragon. Both continue to give me new insight on how to support the investigative potential of young children.

It was entirely by chance that I sat next to Connie Norgren in the PS 321 auditorium in September 1968. We were both nervously waiting for our first staff meeting to begin and we have been friends and teaching soul mates ever since. I owe much of what I know about joyful teaching and the exhilaration of singing with children to Connie.

It was my good fortune to have worked with teaching assistants who shared their wisdom, energy, and warmth with my classroom community. Thank you, Eslin Hughes, Viola Fredas, Laura Keenan, Barbara Cannizzaro, Anna Hawkins, Emilia Concepcion, Aida Ruiz, Maritza Scroco, and Rohini Thakor.

Over the years I have worked with many wonderful student teachers, some of whom later became my teaching colleagues. Liz O'Connell, Allison Gbaje, Suzie Farrell, Melanie Oser, and Eileen Lynch, it is always a pleasure to visit your classrooms and to speak with you about children and teaching. I'm honored to have had Adele Schroeter as a student teacher, colleague, and friend. She rightfully has become an important leader in New York City public education.

Thank you to the late Ellie Barr. Each time she came to observe her student teachers, I noticed a twinkle in her warm eyes as she sat in the corner of the block center, observing the builders and jotting down lots of notes. Ellie loved children. Through many changing tides, she stood strong in her support of play and exploration.

Parents are the most important first teachers in a child's life and I've had the pleasure of getting to know these significant people. Many remain my friends even though their children, my former students, have grown up and had children of their own. It goes without saying that none of this book could have been written if not for the hundreds of children in my life over the years. It's because of them that I know the importance of a day filled with song, investigation, conversation, experimentation, and, of course, play.

Peter Névraumont has been my go-to person whenever I had any questions about the writing and publishing process. I thank him for being a consistent source of encouragement and information.

Kathy Collins and Matt Glover are my two shining lights. I am lucky to have these sensitive, smart, and seriously funny friends in my life. Kathy introduced me to Matt, knowing that we would connect with each other, and I can't thank her enough for linking the three of us.

Thank you to Anna Allanbrook and all of the dedicated teachers at the Brooklyn New School who serve as a model of the best of inquiry-based teaching and learning.

Dan Feigelson wisely introduced me to Rhonda Levy, former principal of PS 142 in Manhattan. In her heart, Rhonda knew that her school population would benefit from experiences with inquiry, exploration, and play. She pushed against the tide of early test-prep-based instruction to give her students those opportunities. Bravo to the early childhood teachers at PS 142 who embraced an inquiry approach to instruction and the wonderful children in their classes.

Thanks to Brooke Peters, Michelle Healy, Todd Sutler, and all the teachers and children at the Compass Charter School for enthusiastically sharing their classrooms with me. Laura Scott and her lovely staff made PS 10 into a second home for me.

Nancy Sing-Bock turned PS 51 into an environment filled with *the arts*, and I'm thrilled to include photographs of her students in this book. Special thanks to Deana Lindner, Megan Ryan, and Giselle Leon for their time and generosity.

I've always wanted to visit the Manhattan New School, and when Mary Anne Sacco invited me to visit her class during choice time, I jumped at the opportunity. The concentration, joy, and involvement of her second graders made me understand why Mary Anne and the Manhattan New School are held in such high esteem.

Working with Lucy Calkins, I learned about the great potential even young kindergarten children have as writers. It was exciting to introduce my young students to a constructivist approach to writing workshop.

I feel absolutely honored to call the distinguished progressive educator Deborah Meier my friend. She has, with great dignity, held fast to her beliefs about the importance of schools being centers of democracy and respect.

I draw inspiration from the work of the children and teachers in Reggio Emilia. Thank you to Lella Gandini for keeping the work alive in the United States.

Special thanks go to Julie Diamond, Fretta Reitzes, and Betsy Grob for their strong belief in learner-centered classrooms.

My meetings with Pat Lynch, Shelley Grant, and Vicki Vinton burst with excitement as we related stories about our mutual passion for our profession.

There are so many people who have helped and inspired me. This is truly only a partial list. Thank you to Ellin Keene, Herb Bleich, Lindsay Shea, Brian Cambourne, Jerome Bruner, Heidi Mills, Neil deGrasse Tyson, Joan Almon, Edward Miller, Sir Ken Robinson, Aiden Chambers, Bobbi Fisher, Lilian Katz, Susan Ochshorn, Tomasen Carey, Scott Filkins, Nakoley Renville, Carl Anderson, Dana Roth, Mayra Rios, Marlene Ross, Chris Napolitan, Wendy Sawyer, Katie Mullaney, Amy Binin, Cheryl Tyler, Hanna Schneewind, Laura Kates, Stacy Mazzone, Katie Rust-Brown, Kori Goldberg, Maryann Laborda, Andy Mastin, Mary Ellen Musacchia, Maureen Morris, Sally O'Connell, Rosa Casiello O'Day, Brooke Peters, Robert Groff, Tu Harris, Mandy Vadnai, and Denise Levine.

The members of my book club, Patricia Tanzosh, Randy Levine Skurnick, Silvia Giliotti, and Ann Carlson, kept me grounded and in good humor as I was working on this book.

Thank you, Spela Sperle, Lisa Primich, and Richard Levine, for keeping my mind and body ready and able to work all year.

Kristin Eno combined her love of children and her wonderful skills as a photographer to take many of the beautiful photos that illustrate the book. Shelley Grant, Bill Fulbrecht, and Pam Kosove generously gave up personal time to take many of the other photos.

I want to thank the wonderful team at Heinemann for all the care they gave to this project: to Alan Huisman for undertaking the challenge of tightening up my meandering sentences, to Vicki Kasabian for her sensitive care in tying together all the parts of the book so beautifully, to Amanda Bondi for her meticulous help in being sure that I handed in materials on time (I know it was a challenge, Amanda!), to Eric Chalek for his patience in helping to arrive at just the right title, to Elizabeth Silvis for helping to bring the book out to the world and to Suzanne Heiser for designing a cover that speaks to the heart of choice time.

I've been privileged to have two incredible editors to lean on during the process of writing this book. Zoë Ryder White was my major advocate and she nurtured me when I needed it, and nudged me when that was important, giving me gentle but wise suggestions. If not for Zoë, I don't know if I would have attempted to undertake this writing project. I can't thank her enough for her friendship and her guidance. When Zoë's beautiful twins were born, Katie Wood Ray took over for her. I've admired Katie from afar for years and, truthfully, was anxious about living up to her standards. What I didn't know was that besides being a brilliant editor, Katie is also gentle, sensitive, and extremely respectful of the writer's intentions. Thank you to my two wonderful editors!

An aunt once told me that families are important in a very special way because they hold the memories of childhood. Thank you to my two sisters, Margaret Forbes and Felice Sudler, holders of many childhood memories.

My bright, talented, and loving daughter, Simone, has brought so much joy to my life. Her unending dedication to her family, her career as a pianist, and her commitment to bringing music into schools throughout the country make my heart swell with gratitude. The place that Jeremy Greensmith, Simone's husband, holds in my life is much more than that of a son-in-law. Jeremy is a compassionate friend in the best sense of the word. He is a talented, much admired teacher and a loving father to my grandson, Adrian. It has been a special gift to be Adrian's grandmother, watching him develop into a talented, thoughtful young man who observes and internalizes the world around him, from the Michelangelo frescoes in the Vatican to the films of James Dean and the music of Bill Evans.

I have no doubt that my life would have been quite different if I had not met Simon Dinnerstein. Together we have visited many art museums, shared our love of cinema, gone to concerts and plays, and spent hours sitting around our dining room table talking about books, music, and always politics. I've reluctantly learned to *almost* love basketball and he has come to share my passion for early childhood education. Simon's sensitivity, his amazing dedication to his art, and his desire to experience and devour all that he can from life have been my inspiration.

Works Cited

Ackerman, Diane. 2000. *Deep Play*. New York: Random House.

Billmeyer, Rachel. 2009. "Creating Thoughtful Readers Through Habits of Mind." In *Habits of Mind Across the Curriculum*, edited by Arthur L. Costa and Bena Kallick, 115–134. Alexandria, VA: Association for Supervision and Curriculum Development. http://www.ascd.org/publications/books/108014/chapters/Creating-Thoughtful-Readers-Through-Habits-of-Mind.aspx.

Brosterman, Norman. 1997. *Inventing Kindergarten*. New York: Abrams.

Brown, Stuart. 2010. *Play: How It Shapes the Brain, Opens the Imagination, and Invigorates the Soul.* With Christopher Vaughan. New York: Avery.

Burns, Marilyn. 2007. *About Teaching Mathematics: A K–8 Resource*. 3rd ed. White Plains, NY: Math Solutions.

Burton, Judith. 2015. "Teaching the Arts to the Children of New York City." In *Blueprint for Teaching and Learning in Visual Arts, Grades PreK to 12*. 3rd ed. New York: New York City Department of Education. http://schools.nyc.gov/offices/teachlearn/arts/files/Blueprints/VisualArts/Blueprint%20for%20Teaching%20and%20Learning%20in%20Visual%20Arts%20June%202015.pdf.

Butler, Sandra. 2016. "Art Abounds at Creativity Festival." *The Durango* (Colo.) *Herald*, March 17. Available at http://www.durangoherald.com/article/20160317/COLUMNISTS54/160319610.

Calkins, Lucy. 2000. *The Art of Teaching Reading*. Portsmouth, NH: Heinemann.

Cambourne, Brian. 1988. *The Whole Story: Natural Learning and the Acquisition of Literacy in the Classroom*. New York: Scholastic.

Campbell, Joseph. 1988. *The Power of Myth*. With Bill Moyers. New York: Doubleday.

Cazden, Courtney. 2001. *Classroom Discourse: The Language of Teaching and Learning*. Portsmouth, NH: Heinemann.

Chambers, Aiden. 1996. *The Reading Environment: How Adults Help Children Enjoy Books.* Portland, ME: Stenhouse.

Cohen, Dorothy. 1988. *The Learning Child: Guidelines for Parents and Teachers*. New York: Schocken Books.

Collins, Kathy, and Matt Glover. 2015. *I Am Reading: Nurturing Young Children's Meaning Making and Joyful Engagement with Any Book*. Portsmouth, NH: Heinemann.

Colman, David. 2008. "Long Before Legos, Wood Was Nice and Did Suffice." *New York Times*, February 10, 11.

Costa, Arthur, and Bena Kallick. 2009. *Habits of Mind Across the Curriculum: Practical and Creative Strategies for Teachers*. Alexandria, VA: Association for Supervision and Curriculum Development.

Cullinan, Bea. 2007. *Read to Me: Raising Kids Who Love to Read.* New York: Scholastic.

Dahl, Roald. 2001. *Charlie and the Glass Elevator*. New York: Random House Children's Books.

Devlin, Keith. 1997. *Mathematics: The Science of Patterns: The Search for Order in Life, Mind, and the Universe.* New York: Henry Holt.

Duncan, Greg J., Chantelle J. Dowsett, Amy Claessens, Katherine Magnuson, Aletha C. Huston, Pamela Klebanov, Linda S. Pagani, Leon Feinstein, Mimi Engel, Jeanne Brooks-Gunn, Holly Sexton, Kathryn Duckworth, and Crista Japel. 2007. "School Readiness and Later Achievement." *Developmental Psychology* 43 (6): 1428–46. http://dx.doi.org/10.1037/0012-1649.43.6.1428.

Edson, Marcia Talhelm. 2013. *Starting with Science: Strategies for Introducing Young Children to Inquiry*. Portland, ME: Stenhouse.

Edwards, Carolyn. 2010. "Three Approaches from Europe: Waldorf, Montessori, and Reggio Emilia." *Early Childhood Research and Practice* 4 (1). Accessed

April 9, 2016, http://www.childcarecanada.org/documents/research-policy-practice/10/10/three-approaches-europe-waldorf-montessori-and-reggio-emilia.

Edwards, Carolyn, Lella Gandini, and George Forman. 1993. *The Hundred Languages of Children: The Reggio Emilia Approach to Early Childhood Education*. Westport, CT: Ablex.

Ernst, Eric. 2014. "Art Review: Surfaces and Substances at Ille Arts." Retrieved from http://hamptonsarthub.com/2014/03/19/surfaces-and-substance-at-ille-arts/.

Gadzikowski, Ann. 2013. *Challenging Exceptionally Bright Children in Early Childhood Classrooms*. St. Paul: Redleaf.

Gardner, Howard. 2011. *Frames of Mind: The Theory of Multiple Intelligences*. New York: Basic Books.

Glover, Matt, and Ellin Oliver Keene. 2015. *The Teacher You Want to Be: Essays About Children, Learning, and Teaching*. Portsmouth, NH: Heinemann.

Harlen, Wynne. 2001. *Primary Science: Taking the Plunge*. 2nd ed. Portsmouth, NH: Heinemann.

Hirsch, Elisabeth S. 1984. *The Block Book*. Washington, DC: National Association for the Education of Young Children.

Hirsh-Pasek, Kathy, and Robert Golinkoff. 2003. *Einstein Never Used Flashcards: How Our Children Really Learn and Why They Need to Play More and Memorize Less*. New York: Rodale Books.

Hirsh-Pasek, Kathy, Robert Golinkoff, Laura Berk, and Dorothy Singer. 2008. *A Mandate for Playful Learning in Preschool: Presenting the Evidence*. New York: Oxford University Press.

Johnston, Peter, and Gay Ivey. 2015. "Engagement: A Hub of Human Development." In *The Teacher You Want to Be: Essays About Children, Learning, and Teaching*, edited by Matt Glover and Ellin Oliver Keene, 50–63. Portsmouth, NH: Heinemann.

Kersétz, André. 1971. *On Reading*. New York: W. W. Norton.

Lee, Joon Sun, and Herbert Ginsburg. 2009. "Early Childhood Teachers' Misconceptions About Mathematics Education for Young Children in the United States." *Australasian Journal of Early Childhood* 34 (4): 37–45.

Meier, Deborah, Brenda S. Engel, and Beth Taylor. 2010. *Playing for Keeps: Life and Learning on a Public School Playground.* New York: Teachers College Press.

Miller, Debbie. 2002. *Reading with Meaning: Teaching Comprehension in the Primary Grades.* Portland, ME: Stenhouse.

Miller, Edward, and Joan Almon. 2009. *Crisis in the Kindergarten: Why Children Need to Play in School.* College Park, MD: Alliance for Childhood.

Mills, Heidi. 2014. *Learning for Real: Teaching Content and Literacy Across the Curriculum.* Portsmouth, NH: Heinemann.

———. 2015. "Why Beliefs Matter." With Tim O'Keefe. In *The Teacher You Want to Be: Essays About Children, Learning, and Teaching*, edited by Matt Glover and Ellin Oliver Keene, 30–49. Portsmouth, NH: Heinemann.

Milne, A. A. 1957. *The World of Pooh: The Complete Winnie-the-Pooh and The House at Pooh Corner.* New York: E. P. Dutton.

Milteer, Regina, Kenneth Ginsburg, and Deborah Ann Mulligan. 2012. "The Importance of Play in Promoting Healthy Child Development and Maintaining Strong Parent–Child Bond: Focus on Children in Poverty." *Pediatrics* 129 (1): 204–13.

Mraz, Kristine, and Marjorie Martinelli. 2014. *Smarter Charts for Math, Science, and Social Studies: Making Learning Visible in the Content Areas K–2.* Portsmouth, NH: Heinemann.

National Association for the Education of Young Children. 2012. *The Common Core State Standards: Caution and Opportunity for Early Childhood Education.* Washington, DC: National Association for the Education of Young Children.

Paley, Vivian Gussin. 1984. *Boys and Girls: Superheroes in the Doll Corner.* Chicago: University of Chicago Press.

———. 2007. "On Listening to What Children Say." *Harvard Educational Review* 77 (2): 152–63.

Phillips, Lisa. 2012. *The Artistic Edge: Seven Skills Children Need to Succeed in an Increasingly Right Brain World.* Toronto: Artistic Edge.

Pratt, Caroline. (1948) 2014. *I Learn from Children: An Adventure in Progressive Education.* New York: Grove.

Pulaski, Mary Ann Spencer. 1970. *Understanding Piaget: An Introduction to Children's Cognitive Development*. New York: Harper and Row.

Randolph, Eleanor. 2011. "The Andy." *The New York Times*, May 13, A18.

Robinson, Sir Ken. 2006. "Do Schools Kill Creativity?" *TED Talks* (podcast), February. Retrieved from http://youtu.be/iG9CE55wbtY.

Sulzby, Elizabeth. 1971. "Assessment of Emergent Literacy: Storybook Reading." *The Reading Teacher* 44 (7): 498–500.

Thérond, Roger. 2001. *Encounters with Great Painters*. New York: Abrams.

Tough, Joan. 1976. *Listening to Children Talking*. London: Ward Lock Educational.

Tyson, Neil deGrasse. 2004. *The Sky Is Not the Limit: Adventures of an Urban Astrophysicist*. New York: Prometheus Books.

Quindlen, Anna. 1998. *How Reading Changed My Life*. New York: Random House.

Venes, Donald. 2009. *Taber's Cyclopedic Medical Dictionary*. 21st ed. Philadelphia: F. A. Davis.

Vygotsky, Lev. 1978. *Mind in Society: The Development of Higher Psychological Processes*. Cambridge, MA: Harvard University Press.

Wood, Chip. 1996. *Yardsticks: Children in the Classroom, Ages 4–14: A Resource for Parents and Teachers*. Greenfield, MA: Northeast Foundation for Children.